ROD BUILDING
AND
R·E·P·A·I·R

LEN HEAD

ILLUSTRATED BY JOHN HOLDEN

THE CROWOOD PRESS

First published in 1984 by
THE CROWOOD PRESS LTD
Ramsbury, Marlborough
Wiltshire SN8 2HR

Paperback edition 1992

British Library Cataloguing in Publication Data

A catalogue record for this book is available from the British Library.

ISBN   1 85223 719 8

Acknowledgements

My thanks go to the following who provided background information or mad
available various rod blanks and accessories discussed in the book:

Ken Draper, North Western Blanks.
John Mitchell, Normark.
Bruce Vaughan, Ryobi Masterline.
Tri Cast Composite Tubes.
Sportex.
Fibatube.
John Bruce of the Swim and Pitch tackle shop.

Special thanks to:
Jack and Roger of that Mecca of fishing tackle Simpson's of Turnford for
their assistance.
Bob Jones for his welcome advice.

Illustrations © John Holden 1984

Typeset by Inforum Ltd, Portsmouth
Printed in Great Britain by Redwood Press Ltd, Melksham, Wilts

CONTENTS

Section 1

ROD BLANK MATERIALS AND THEIR DEVELOPMENT

Modern rod development provides a superb variety of blanks in glassfibre, carbonfibre and composites. The popularity of modest priced hollow glassfibre blanks is rapidly giving way to the superior fishing qualities of carbon and composites. Ordinary glass blanks will disappear in the near future, though in the meantime their low cost makes them worth considering for your first hesitant steps into rod building.

Glass blank development took a stride forward with the relatively recent incorporation of 'S' glass, a higher quality fibre which is lighter, tougher and gives superior blank performance. 'S' glass is used chiefly in surfcasting where its casting power provides excellent blanks almost equal to carbonfibre performance at half the price. Elsewhere in the fishing world, carbon has put an untimely end to the further development of 'S' glass, which otherwise would be found in more fly and freshwater rods of all kinds.

Original carbonfibre rods suffered a few teething problems which resulted in a certain amount of apprehension among fishermen and rod builders. Early breakages were due mainly to inferior resins used to bind the carbonfibre filaments within the blank. Today's rods with Space-age resin binders are much more reliable; buy them with confidence for any kind of fishing – provided you stick with leading brand names.

Carbonfibre or carbon composite is now the automatic choice of experienced anglers and custom rod builders. Rod weight is reduced to about half that of a glassfibre blank of equivalent power and action. The blank's smaller cross-section allows easier, longer and more accurate casting. Striking and line pick-up are quieter and snappier, and hooks are set more efficiently. Playing fish is pure pleasure on a well designed carbonfibre rod.

Perhaps the greatest advantages are in light float and fly rods that are held for an entire fishing session. You can fish all day with an ultra-light carbon rod without suffering any fatigue. And it is superior in other kinds of fishing as well – tench, carp, beachcasting and pike rods cast farther and set hooks more efficiently at long range than fibreglass ever could. The slender tip of a carbonfibre beach blank indicates bites which would remain undetected on other materials.

Several manufacturers now produce composite blanks of carbon/glass, carbon/boron and carbon/aramid mixtures,

Tri-cast's carbon/aramid materials blend lightness and quick response with far greater insurance against overload.

all of which give certain advantages in price, action or strength. Carbon/glass gives middle of the road prices and performance – a useful compromise for many anglers.

A glass beach blank reinforced in the middle with carbonfibre results in a stiffer rod with little extra weight. It casts better but does not cost the earth. Conoflex Flick Tip beach blanks incorporate a glass mixture in the tip section which, it is claimed, offers more flexibility to handle soft baits and tiny bites – similar to a freshwater quiver tip rod. The development of boron fishing rods is still in its infancy with only a few manufacturers testing the water. Boron is even stiffer than carbonfibre, giving the possibility of yet thinner rods for given power. Its cost verges on the prohibitive, and

that is the main deterrent to development. Boron currently is limited to a few fly and freshwater rods, and to special butts for high-performance beachcasting blanks.

Drawbacks of carbonfibre are its fragility and intolerance of overflexing. You can chuck glassfibre rods around, stub the tip into the ground, even shut it in the car door. And it still survives . . . some of the time. Carbonfibre shatters at the slightest knock.

However, modern blank manufacturers now resolve the fragility problem by applying aerospace technology, incorporating aramid fibres with carbon and binding them with high-impact resin. These blanks are resistant to knocks and less likely to snap through overload whilst retaining most f the advantages of good carbonfibre.

Carbonfibre and carbonfibre composites, then, are recommended as first choice for the home rod builder. Do not be guided by price and appearances alone though: it is simple enough for the crafty manufacturer to give cheap, inferior blanks a smooth, glossy surface finish with plenty of sales appeal. Be suspicious of all very low price blanks claimed to offer full carbonfibre performance specifications.

'100 per cent carbon' is the most misleading description of all. No rod can be totally carbonfibre. All blanks are wrapped on to an underlay of glassfibre scrim, and every one is bonded by resins. Forget percentage figures. Instead, choose a blank according to weight, power, action and, most importantly, reputation.

Unfortunately, a loophole in our marketing laws allows blanks and rods from Korea and Taiwan to be imported and sold here without the country of origin being marked in any way. It is also unfortunate that the general angling public cannot easily differentiate between good and low quality carbonfibre blanks; and of course it is impossible to assess the resins without laboratory tests.

Most, if not all, cheap Far Eastern blanks are inferior in quality and performance, factors difficult to define until after you have bought, built and fished with the rod. Only then do you discover it lacks good carbon's sparkle and reliability. Many of them break prematurely.

Throughout these pages the emphasis is on good quality materials. Why waste your time on rubbish? The only safe way is to

Specialist dealers offer an overwhelming selection of blanks, kits and part-built rods.

select blanks and accessories from our leading manufacturers and distributors. Some of them do handle imported blanks, but are hardly likely to risk their reputations on trash. You can buy with full confidence.

Time is never wasted by testing blanks beforehand. Admittedly, opportunities to do so are uncommon; not many tackle dealers have demonstration rods to offer – hardly surprising considering the huge range available and new designs arriving all the time. But there are fishing conferences, tackle shows, game fairs and tackle demonstrations held all over the country. Most have test facilities available. Better still, ask around your friends and borrow a rod if you can. At least that way you learn who your real friends are.

More often than not, a visit to a well known specialist shop – Simpsons of Turnford, Alan Brown of Hitchin, Terry Eustace in Birmingham and Breakaway Tackle of Ipswich amongst others – will reveal all the answers and provide an opportunity to waggle dozens of blanks.

It has been said that all in-shop tests are meaningless; that you have to get out to the water and actually fish with a rod to get a true evaluation. Disregard any such comments as nonsense. You cannot fish with a blank until you have bought and built it, so in the absence of test facilities waggling the blank or hanging on to the butt while the dealer pulls the tip well past its test curve at least give you some idea of action and power.

Test curves are determined by finding the weight required to pull the tip down to right angles to the butt. Anchor the butt to floor or wall, tie a short piece of line to the tip, and form a loop in the far end. Hitch the loop to a spring balance and then drag the tip around until the line lies at right angles to the butt section of the blank. Read off the pull weight

registered on the balance: that is the test curve rating.

Optimum casting weight in ounces of any blank is proportional to its test curve in pounds. A 1 lb test curve allows 1 oz to be cast, and so on. Multiply the test curve figure by 5 to calculate ideal line breaking strain for the rod. The 1 lb test curve is ideally matched to 5 lb line. Both casting weight and line strength can be safely extended by about 50 per cent from basic.

However, in some ways test curves are an arbitrary guide to a blank's power. Two independent testers can easily arrive at different ratings depending on their interpretation of the precise tip position relative to the butt when the blank is under pressure. A small deviation either side of right angles causes considerable variation in test readings.

Different action blanks may have identical test curves but still feel entirely different in your hands. Fast tapered blanks seem far more powerful than a comparable slow blank.

Arbitrary as it is, the test curve is still a useful yardstick of blank power and is used by manufacturers to designate the suitability of their products for various kinds of fishing.

Bare blanks feel deceptively stiffer than they are when rings and fittings are added. This is particularly true of long, light floatfishing blanks. The extra mass of rings softens the action in the rod's upper half. Allow for that by choosing a blank slightly harder than the finished rod you prefer.

Virtually all blanks and kits arrive with factory fitted spigot joints. You may come across one with a poor fit, but generally speaking they are all made to precise tolerances. There is nothing to be gained by making your own joints. A well fitted spigot should have a gap of about ¼ inch when the sections are pushed together to allow for

Avoid the common mistake of choosing too powerful a rod. Balance the blank's length and test curve to the general run of fish. All good rods will still land that elusive monster.

Southend boat fisherman Harry Evans hooked his 32lb cod on light uptide tackle. A badly engineered spigot would have snapped like matchwood.

wear and tear. There should be no trace of knocking or clicking when the assembled blank is flicked from side to side. Any sound indicates a poorly milled joint or a loose male spigot.

You could buy or specially order a one piece blank to cut and spigot for yourself. There are distinct problems though: spigot taper, material, wall thickness and overlap must be matched to the blank itself. You would have to rely on the dealer finding a suitable plug section for you, and that is almost impossible.

Long casting blanks may perform better by cutting and spigotting to produce a long tip and short butt, but transportation difficulties cancel out the advantages to the extent that it is better, taking everything into consideration, to stick to the equal length section formula. I have omitted details of spigotting mechanics from this section because I believe most rod builders do better to buy a ready jointed blank.

Some manufacturers have introduced a new type of joint called 'Overfit', which is claimed to give a superior through-action while doing away with the fuss of cutting and glueing a conventional spigot. These blanks are made by rolling each section on a separate mandrel so that the bottom of the tip section pushes directly over the male end of the butt.

The method meets with some criticisms: it looks wrong aesthetically, detracts from action, and is simply a means of reducing manufacturing costs. Overfit certainly does not look as neat as a spigot, but I do not think that most reputable manufacturers would ake the risk of producing inferior blanks this way. Fenwick, America's leading rod company, uses the similar but technically more advanced Feralite system on all their rods from light fly to heavy surf.

A few tests in the tackle shop prove that action is not affected. Early Sportex designs were a problem because the blank had not been reinforced in the lower joint to compensate for reduced diameter. This has been corrected by extra wraps of material which improve action and smoothness in the overfit area.

Does an overfit spigot last as long as the conventional joint? Time will tell of course, but I have used rods for two years with as yet no sign of spigot wear. Fenwick's Feralite system has been marketed for over a decade, and some of the original blanks are still hard at work. Indeed, the Feralite spigot is specially calculated to compensate for wear in the blank walls, and in theory should have an unlimited service life.

Once you buy a new blank, you are stuck with it. So here are a few final pointers to bear in mind before parting with your cash. Blanks are not consistently good by any means; even the leading factories suffer the occasional lapse through poor quality con-

trol. Watch out for blanks with uneven wall thickness, a fairly common problem which can be spotted by checking the bottom of the tip and both ends of the butt. Walls should be even throughout the blank's circumference. If not, look for another.

Check the full length for hairline cracks which are especially noticeable in thin walls. Consider that a coat of paint can hide all sorts of nasties; and in any case, paint is superfluous on high-quality glass and carbon. Reject painted carbonfibre blanks as a matter of course unless you are absolutely convinced of the maker's pedigree. Stick with plain black or brown self-coloured blanks which reveal the surface weave of the impregnated cloth. Burgundy and green carbonfibre blanks are a viable option – here again the colouration is part of the resin system, not a lick of paint.

Few blanks are absolutely straight. A slight bend seen at the tip is nothing to worry about. Most good blanks will have one anyway. But beware of a sudden, pronounced diversion in the walls which may be accompanied by broken fibres, bubbles, or hairline cracks. These are serious defects which guarantee big trouble for the careless rod builder.

Section 2

CHOOSING A PERFECT BLANK FOR HOME BUILDING

There are so many blanks on the market that choosing one can be a perplexing business unless you have some idea of what you need. Beginners are at a special disadvantage, and even professional builders are advised to think hard before investing. Exactly what length, action, power and type of rod do you prefer?

Surely, all you need is a general purpose fishing rod? Not so, I'm afraid. There are rods described as general purpose but which in reality span a narrow gap.

This is not to say that all general purpose blanks are useless; far from it. But to fish properly for a chosen species at a chosen range with preset limits on line breaking strain, the blank must be more closely matched to the job than generality allows. Not long ago I saw an angler gamely trying to catch roach from a small stream using curly 18 lb line and a 7 ft boat fishing rod – tackle totally unsuited to species and conditions. He had caught nothing, and stood no chance of success.

RODS FOR FRESHWATER AND FLY FISHING

Float rods for roach, etc

Float fishing for roach is a good place to begin this investigation of rod and blank types. Roach are the most common and most fished for species in the country, and rods suited to them will also be suitable for other small species such as dace and average size bream. Go for a blank between 12 and 13 ft long, which is the perfect length range for floatfishing except in the occasional situation where a 14 footer offers certain advantages, of which more later.

Roach fishing often demands delicate bait presentation on fine lines and tiny hooks. Since biting fish can be finicky, fast striking is called for, and the result of this is a broken hook length unless the rod tip is soft enough to cushion the nylon. Look for a blank with a flexible tip to absorb shock, progressive

Trotting for roach with Normark's NMB-156 carbon blank made up into a 13ft float rod.

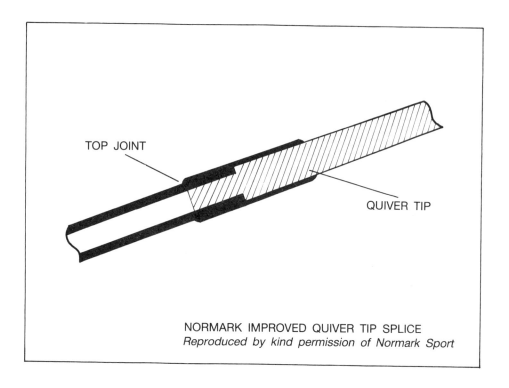

TOP JOINT

QUIVER TIP

NORMARK IMPROVED QUIVER TIP SPLICE
Reproduced by kind permission of Normark Sport

action below it, and a fairly stiff middle and butt to allow good casting, perfect tackle control and sufficient backbone to play fish. Such a blank has ample power in reserve if you should hook a big fish. Many match type blanks are designed with this work in mind.

On regularly fished waters, fish become much more difficult to tempt, so that very fine lines and hook lengths down to $\frac{3}{4}$ lb breaking strain or less must be used along with corresponding minute hooks. To make rods even more sensitive to such frail tackle, rod designers splice in ultra-light tip sections 15–20 ins long.

If you intend to use these fine lines, choose a blank with a spliced tip, but it is important to check that the tip is correctly tapered and jointed to blend with the lower sections. The bent rod should assume a smooth curve and not be stepped or doglegged at the splice.

Slightly more powerful blanks are necessary to punch out heavy wagglers and higher breaking strain lines cast to longer ranges. Choose a blank that will handle lines up to 4 lbs B.S. and hook lengths down to 1½ lbs. A snappy-action 13 footer casts well, gives good tackle control and will pick up line from long ranges.

The three rods described cope with most float work in still waters and for trotting in slow-moving rivers and canals. For trotting faster rivers, however, a more progressive, through-actioned blank will prove to be better.

Striking and playing relatively small fish

upstream through heavy currents places considerable strain on your tackle. Using a stiff rod in these conditions is likely to result in either breaking off on the strike or having the hook tear out as you fight the fish. The rod is not forgiving enough in action to absorb the combined pressure of current and fish. A slower-actioned blank with plenty of response in the middle reacts perfectly to the load, cushioning the plunges of a lively fish and retaining a safe hookhold, as well as enhancing the enjoyment to be gained from this type of fishing. The best available are 12 ft Avon Trotters from Simpson's of Turnford or from Terry Eustace Rods and Blanks.

Earlier I mentioned a 14 ft float rod. One advantage of extra length is to enable easier fishing over marginal weed. You can also fish a fixed float at greater depth.

Specialist blanks up to 15 ft are sold by Normark and up to 19 ft by Bruce & Walker Limited.

But it is to trotting that I refer mainly. One of the arts of good trotting is to hold back the float's progress downstream, and this is much easier and more effective if the float travels along a direct line from the rod tip. A 14 ft rod is valuable here because it holds line farther from the bank.

If a 14 ft rod is better than the standard 12–13 ft one, why not use 15 or 20 ft? As rods grow longer they become increasingly more unbalanced and unpleasant to handle. Even carbon rods are a handful. Indeed, some anglers refuse to go beyond 13 ft at all costs. However, I can only say that you should at least try a longer rod before making your final decision. They do have their uses.

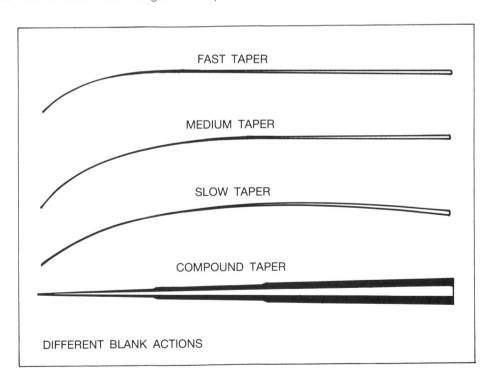

FAST TAPER

MEDIUM TAPER

SLOW TAPER

COMPOUND TAPER

DIFFERENT BLANK ACTIONS

Leger rods for roach, etc

Here again the blank must be matched to conditions. Test curve rating is a practical guide to leger rod assessment. If you intend to fish big stillwaters with blockends, swimfeeders and heavy leads, look at blanks around 11 ft long with a ¾–1¼ lb test curve. Progressive tip and middle sections assist casting and cushion tackle from sudden snatches which might otherwise rip off soft baits or prematurely empty the feeder. The action also permits safe fishing with lighter lines and hook lengths, yet the stiffish butt still develops enough power for fairly long casting.

Such blanks are perfect for pulling in big roach and bream at ranges of up to 40 yds. Beyond that, it is necessary to step up the test curve rating to the tench specification described later, though using more powerful rods than those described will certainly take some of the pleasure out of your fishing since roach and bream are not powerful fighters. Enticing them closer and using lighter tackle may be the better option.

Swing tip blanks

Special swing tip blanks of smooth, progressive action for fine line work, are readily available, but they are mostly on the short side – up to 8½ ft. These are adequate for close fishing and have some merit in allowing a better view of the tip itself. An extra 12–18 ins is hardly less sensitive but would give much superior line pick-up and more versatility for longer range fishing.

Roach caught on long-range swimfeeder tackle at Arleigh Reservoir, Essex.

A spliced-in quiver tip should blend with the main blank's action. Ringing pattern must be spot-on.

Quiver tip spliced leger rods

Separate screw-in quiver and swing tips are used on virtually any leger rod. They thread on to the tip ring and can be changed in a moment to match currents and conditions. Their drawback is that they detract from the rod's feel and do nothing for its casting action. A quiver tip, on the other hand, is a joy to fish with, giving superior bite detection, much better casting and a smooth action for playing fish on light lines. The tip enhances the rod's feel in hand.

A spliced quiver tip is either part of the top joint or a separate piece added on to the main blank. Well designed quiver rods curve so smoothly that you cannot readily detect the joint by appearance and action alone.

The problem lies in blending a fine, sensitive quiver into the top of an ordinary rod blank. Normark's answer is to do away with the splice and to roll the quiver into the main blank instead, as part of the manufacturing process. An additional wrap of carbonfibre applied over the joint area produces a tell-tale parallel section rather than the traditional and unsightly bulge.

Some manufactuers incorporate interchangeable quiver tips of varying tapers which slot into the top joint to cope with changing conditions. I have yet to try them, but hear excellent reports. If your fishing demands a blank action that is not available on the open market, making your own quiver rod presents no great problem.

A majority of the best match fishermen prefer rods with built-in or detachable quiver tips. These rods are perfect for general fishing as well.

Tench rods

Float fishing for tench seems to have lost favour to some extent, which is a pity. Some of the most enjoyable and exciting sport is in tangling with big, float-caught fish hooked close in. The nicest float rod for tench has a compound action right down to the butt, so that you feel the fish's every move. Conditions permitting, it is the best choice of all.

Very often though it is necessary to place baits amid or alongside weedbeds, where hooked tench bolt, given half a chance. More powerful blanks are essential to keep them out. Middle-to-tip action with some power in the butt casts well, feels reasonably good with a fish on, and holds enough strength in reserve to bully a big tench. 12 ft rods are about right, though 13

footers allow deeper swims to be float fished without sliders. Blanks of the correct length and action are rare — a reflection of declining popularity.

If you cannot afford carbonfibre, Simpson's of Turnford offer the Tenchfisher, a new glassfibre blank either $11\frac{1}{2}$ or 12 ft long. The longer rod is well suited to heavier styles of tench float fishing and would double up as a trotter for fast currents holding barbel and chub.

Short range fishing through a gap in marginal reeds is another common tench scenario. Marginal weeds present similar problems. Upon feeling the hook, tench surge headlong into the nearest obstruction. For some reason a direct overhead pull disconcerts the fish; it does not know which way to run and becomes more controllable. A longer rod than described above — say

Sportex's Avon blank, test curve 1lb punches swimfeeders and leger tackle far enough to suit general tench requirements.

15 ft long — would put many margin weedbed tench on the bank.

You must hold them hard though; quite a task considering the leverage a big tench exerts on such a long blank. Anything longer than 15 ft would not develop sufficient line tension.

I have used a 15½ ft beast of a float rod which served well until a cow trod on it. It was made from sections of roach pole. Assembling your own blank is for most anglers the only solution. Rod and blank makers seldom cater for such limited demand. Normark, however, supply a 15 ft specialist float rod with a 1 lb test curve (ref. NMVB180—3). They claim it will handle lines of up to 4 lbs breaking strain, but actually you can use 6 lbs with confidence. As you lean into the tench, the more powerful mid-sections of blank are drawn into play. Alternatively, look at some of the lighter salmon fly fishing blanks. Most could be adapted for float work.

Powerful rods and heavy lines are unnecessary in clean water. Where tench will accept biggish baits, the through action rod first described, matched to 4 lb line, can strike home a decent size hook and feels exceptionally nice during the battle. Unfortunately, tench in snag free waters are particularly cagey, so it is usually important to fine down your tackle. Use small hooks, light lines and floats shotted down to indicate the merest tweak of a bite.

In this situation through action is worse than useless. It does not have the fast line pick-up necessary to dot those tiny bites. For a more suitable rod, choose a fine tip, fast-action 13 ft match blank. Do not be concerned about their apparent lack of power. Power is there when it is needed. And in any case, remember that the rod is recommended for fine float fishing in clear waters where there is plenty of room to play a fish . . . and no excuse for being broken.

Leger and feeder rods

Blank selection depends on whether the rod is used for close-to-medium work or for long ranges up to 70 yds. For extreme range, refer to the carp section (*see* pages 17–22). Close-to-medium range leger and feeder rods for tench, chub, bream and barbel may be built from a wide range of blanks produced by nearly all major factories. They are described as Avons.

A compound taper Avon of 11–11¼ ft, and test curve 1 lb, handles lines between 3 and 6 lbs test, is very pleasant to fish with at ranges of up to 35 yards with and without feeders, and has all the response you could ask for when a fish is hooked. Few, if any, blanks are as versatile as Avons, which serve equally well for legering for the species mentioned and for fishing barbel and chub in fast water, trotting style.

Manufacturers' interpretations of Avon action range from soft and sloppy to firm, stepped-up power. You will not go far wrong with North Western, Fibatube and Sportex. The Sportex CA3351 in carbonfibre, 11 ft long and test curve 1 lb, is the most versatile blank I have ever used. It is superb at close-to-medium ranges.

Do not disregard that really soft blank which bends right through to its handle. It can greatly increase the number of tench hooked from tight weed and snaggy swims. A thicker walled but soft through-action of 1¼ lbs test curve is ideal. Load your reel with 7 lb line, screw down the drag and switch on the anti-reverse. When you hook a tench, hold the rod low and pull hard. The fish will not break your line. It bounces around on the end and wears itself out against the limber blank.

Beginners to this game of allowing tench to bounce around on the end of a limber rod may well lose their cool and yield line from the reel spool. If you, too, doubt the effectiveness of the method go into the garden, tie the line to a post, or something similar, then pull. You will discover that it is almost impossible to break the 7lb B.S. line, and completely impossible to break a line that is just a couple of pounds stronger.

Fast taper rods are very much in fashion for longer range heavier lead and swimfeeder work. They *could* be right for you. Although there is no denying the problems of casting the required distance and setting the hook with such rods, they are more efficient than slower actioned rods. But they are less than perfect for three reasons.

Their poker-stiff action transmits little feel of the fish to your hands. The unforgiving tip can easily bump a fish clean off the hook as it nears the bank, whereas a softer rod would absorb those sudden shocks. And fast taper rods are nowhere near as versatile: more a problem for anglers on limited budgets than for the man who can afford to indulge in a rod for every specialist department, perhaps, but still a factor to be considered.

Carp rods

The vast range of carp fishing blanks does not include even one for float fishing, as far as I am aware. What little float fishing takes place is carried out by adding a float to whatever rod happens to be available at the time. Carp takes are relatively few and far between, and it is just not feasible to sit watching a float for hours on end — even if there were advantages in doing so.

Sometimes a group of fish are around the bait but modern end rigs produce nothing apart from twitches too small to hit on conventional tackle. In that case, a float rod does have serious applications. Dropping big, heavily shotted floats on to the head of a feeding carp is not a good idea, so these specialist rods would need to cast light tackle yet still have the speed and power to pick up line, drive in the hook and handle a big fish. A 13 footer of $1\frac{1}{2}$ lb test curve seems right.

So much nonsense is talked about carp rods that anyone equipping himself can be forgiven for believing the need for half a dozen pairs of the latest super-duper designs. In fact, four different types of rod cover just about every situation. They are a general purpose workhorse, a long range rod, a snag fishing rod and an optional extreme range caster.

A versatile workhorse can be made from a compound taper blank 11 ft long and $1\frac{3}{4}$ lb test curve. Pick a blank with action through the tip and middle, progressing into a firmer butt. You will find it ideal for most margin, short and medium range fishing with floaters, particles and bottom baits; and although it feels good with a small carp on the end it has the power necessary to control a heavy specimen. The blanks match 6–11 lb lines and 1–$1\frac{1}{2}$ oz leads, but will lob 2 ozs beyond 80 yds when pressed.

If longer range is necessary, choose a fast tapered 11–12 ft blank tested at 2–$2\frac{1}{2}$ lbs. Slightly less powerful rods which combine excellent casting power with easy handling and versatility can be found in the Simpson's of Turnford KMDT series, Terry Eustace's L/R carbons and the Rod Hutchinson range. All these blanks are of long casting compound design, a good choice for enjoyable carp fishing.

Snag fishing for carp means screwing the reel clutch tight and not giving an inch of line, or you will lose fish. For tench fishing I

'Bouncing' a carp in snaggy water.

described a soft action blank useful for holding on hard in snags and weeds. The same comments apply to carp, only more so. The rod must be considerably more powerful – a thick walled, slow action which you can feel through to the handle when the blank is fully flexed. At 10 ft long, the rod is shorter than most modern carp blanks in order to increase its pulling power. Match the rod to 15 lb Sylcast line and let the carp bounce around against its $2–2\frac{1}{2}$ lb test curve.

One current demand for big water fishing is the ability to cast a boilie ever and ever farther to where carp feed. Manufacturers respond with increasingly powerful, faster tapered blanks. In my view this approach is wrong. A walk around a carp lake shows that most anglers use a stunted casting action where the rod is held horizontally behind and snapped over in a short power arc in which little more than the tip of the rod is brought into play. The middle and butt are untapped.

A fast taper rod with its power at the tip is undoubtedly the best design for achieving good distances with an overhead thump. It is an accurate if not too powerful casting method at home in overgrown swims without the space for more powerful styles.

Some casters prefer a layback cast which gains extra distance because the rod is compressed harder throughout its power stroke. But the style is still too inefficient to wind up a powerful modern carbonfibre blank.

Not all carp swims restrict your style. Many of the big gravel pits, where long range is vital, have plenty of space for an improved pendulum cast; and if that method

Long distance fishing has a strong impact on rod design. Are today's carp rod designers on the right track, or is there a better way?

is coupled to a specially designed casting blank, perhaps with a semi-rigid butt and progressive mid-section, it should be possible to sling a boilie where no boilie has been slung before. Building a rod to reach ultra-long distances is certainly feasible; indeed, it has already been achieved in a few models and by a few rod makers. If the distance an outfit will cast is the only consideration, why not go down to the lake armed with a fast-actioned powerful beachcaster of carbon, or even boron, and a supply of 5 and 6 oz leads, then let fly at the horizon? But, of course, distance is not the only consideration, for carp fishing with beasts of rods like that would take all the pleasure out of the fight. Even a big carp would be unable to give a proper account of itself.

Far superior would be a blank of stepped or 'zoned' design and taper, perhaps 12 ft 6 in long and 2¾ lbs T.C., made with low-modulus carbon in the tip to give plenty of 'feel' – especially close in; a composite of boron and carbon in the middle section, and high modulus in the butt for great casting power. Such a rod, coupled with a powerful casting style, would achieve formidable distances, while losing nothing in the playing of the carp.

Pike rods

Gone are the days when an old boat or sea fishing rod doubled up for piking. Outlooks and techniques have changed for the better and with them come a range of specialist blanks for all kinds of pike fishing.

Like carp blanks, pike models can be divided into those for close-to-medium fishing and for long range. In fact, the more powerful carp blanks will double up for piking too. For most pike fishing you need a blank with a slow to medium action, test curve 2½–3 lbs and 11–12 ft long.

Fast action rods are a poor choice if most of your pike fishing involves work with soft deadbaits and big livebaits. A fast rod rips hooks out of baits during the cast. Soft baits can be lobbed a surprising distance with a through action rod, which can confidently be used with a wide variety of techniques including legering, freelining, suspended or float legering, float paternoster and trotting. It will cast a frozen mackerel up to 80 yards.

If you must use very big baits, fish near submerged branches, or on the big pike waters in Ireland and Scotland, step up the test curve to 3½ lbs.

Some anglers prefer medium fast rods. They are not so enjoyable to use and extra care is essential if you are to avoid tearing hooks out of the bait. But they are versatile enough to be considered an alternative to the standard rod, and in addition will cast a very long way with small baits.

Fast taper can be recommended only when extreme casting range holds the key to success, and only then for throwing very small deadbaits and 2–3 oz of lead. You certainly don't need the brisk action for picking up line and striking. The best way to hook a pike is to wind up tight and bend the rod into it – a medium action rod does that to perfection.

Vane float fishing is growing popular. Deadbaits drift out with the wind so far that you can hardly see the float.

A very solid rod is necessary for winding down on pike at such long ranges, hence the popularity of bass rods. Longer rods than those currently on sale would improve line control. Obviously one could not expect miracles at 150–200 yds, but a 13 ft blank would be more effective than a short one. It might not offer the best fighting qualities but in this case the name of the game is to hook your fish in the first place.

Boat rods for pike fishing

Standard pike rods can be used at a push but through action is even better for playing a good fish under the boat. Its forgiving nature prevents the hooks bouncing out of the fish's jaws. Working space is limited aboard a dinghy laden with anglers and tackle, so long rods can be a nuisance; 10 ft is a realistic length, perhaps even 11 ft, but anything much longer is likely to prove more of a handicap than a help.

Fly rods

Fly rod power is calculated according to AFTM ratings. The lower the number, the lighter the line and vice versa. A well equipped trout fisherman needs a variety of rods for different waters and varying conditions on any given water. A trip to Rutland or Grafham reservoirs could mean long-casting lures and heavy sinking line into strong winds. It takes a stiff AFTM 8 or 9 blank, 9–9½ ft long to shoot a long line and drive home the hook.

Later in the evening, or in a quiet backwater, trout may feed on sub-surface pupae or hatching flies – conditions totally unsuitable for powerful rods and shooting heads. It takes a very skilful caster to drop a heavy shooting head onto the water gently enough not to scare trout. Light, delicate tackle is a wise choice. A popular choice might be a 9 ft, slow actioned rod, balanced to AFTM 5–7 floating line. That way you can cast a wider loop more accurately and achieve thistledown delivery of fly and line. Many reservoir anglers carry two outfits to cover these extremes.

Broadly speaking, the rougher the conditions, the higher your line rating must be. Reservoir boat anglers exposed to the worst of the elements often choose very powerful rods 10 ft long and AFTMA 10 weight. Some prefer a light carp blank made up for trolling big lures and to cast heavy sinking heads and lead core line.

The modern stocking policy on smaller put-and-take waters is to use big trout. Where you are likely to latch into one, equip yourself with an outfit similar to that used on reservoirs. Converted carp blanks are unnecessary, but you do need the muscle of an AFTM 8–9 blank throwing a weight forward floating line. The blank will be useful for sunk line fishing as well, but this is an uncommon technique on really small waters.

Mighty reservoir or small pond, there is nothing to match the pure pleasure of nymph fishing with a light wand of a rod and AFTM 4–5 weight line. Such an outfit handles sweetly and presents the fly better. If you have not hooked a big trout on light tackle, you certainly have a treat in store.

It is noticeable that many newcomers to fly fishing choose a heavy blank which later they change for a lighter outfit. Before you buy that heavy blank and spend hours building it into a fine rod, stop and think. Do you really need it for your style of trout fishing?

A slower action 7½–8½ ft AFTM 5, 6 or 7 blank is perfectly suitable for small rivers and streams where accurate casting of double taper lines is required. It is all too easy for hooks to rip out of fighting fit stream trout which have the current in their favour. A slow rod with plenty of easy bend absorbs head shaking jolts and aerial fireworks.

Dapping rods

The casting power of dapping blanks is irrelevant because this style of fishing

Long distance fly casting is a combination of good technique and sufficient line weight to flex the rod right down the handle. Rods that are too stiff never cast properly.

Smooth shooting action drops a fly on the water without scaring the fish.

The traditional fly rod design still preferred by most trout fishermen — scrolled cork handle and screw reel seat.

Lamiglas AFTM5 blank in action. Soft tip-action buffers the leader against the fish's attack.

ntails dapping or dabbling flies from a short ne downwind of a boat or even from the ank. Trout attack violently, so the blank hould not be too stiff. The ideal choice is a oft tipped 12–14 ft blank.

RODS FOR BOAT AND BEACH FISHING

Traditional boat rods

he tackle trade and leading organisations, ed by the International Game Fishing Association, have injected some sanity and tability into the muddled world of rod and lank specification by drawing up a comarative system based on line breaking train. Why pick line? It is easily measured nd forms the backbone of your outfit, since s strength alone determines the useful mits of rod, reel and terminal rig.

12, 20, 30 and 50 lb class blanks are of pecial relevance to our boat fishing, though ghter and heavier classifications exist. 1 theory, blank power should now be neasured in kilograms rather than pounds; owever, even the official body runs a dual neasuring system simply because American anglers – who account for the overvhelming majority of line-class fishermen – esist the shift to metric. It doesn't have nuch of a following here either: just try sking your tackle dealer for 6 kg line and a natching rod.

Use the line class system for convenient omparisons between rods and to draw up a eague table of tackle weight for particular pecies of fish. With those yardsticks, you an select a blank and accessories that nake a sporting outfit for your favourite fish. t isn't the perfect solution, but it at least revents disastrous mistakes like buying a hark rod to catch whiting and dabs.

Line class tackle is based on the traditional boat rod design of glassfibre tip and detachable handle. Overall length varies roughly in step with poundage. $7\frac{1}{2}$–$8\frac{1}{2}$ ft is suitable for the 12 and 20 lb class; 30–50 lb rods are better kept around the 7 ft mark which provides a better leverage ratio when you haul on the line. The shorter the rod, the more impression you make on a fish.

Most boat rods are made from ordinary hollow fibreglass which withstands a good deal of abuse and does not suffer from prolonged exposure to corrosive saltwater. Blank action is usually pitched in the medium-fast bracket, a neat balance between easy handling and efficiency.

It is important that the handle be stiff enough to channel plenty of muscle power to the tip. Even light 12 lb rods benefit from a substantial handle. Butts of flimsy glassfibre absorb much of your effort, produce a soggy feeling, and are liable to break without warning. Thick-walled glassfibre, hightensile aluminium alloy and straight grained wood (ash or hickory) are acceptable. Never compromise on the butt quality of the heavier rods: should a 50 lb rod break under full load, splinters of metal, glass or wood will stab you in the belly.

Even lightweight fishing strains the reel seat. Snap-lock clips and weak screw fittings are useless on a boat rod. Choose a conventional chromed brass reel seat, the Fuji FPS carbonfibre/stainless steel seat or an equivalent. Butt and tip may be jointed under the reel seat, in which case you are better off fitting a Modalock-style ferrule/reel seat which, although heavy, is strong and reliable. Otherwise, pick a spigotted blank and butt, which do not require reinforcement from the reel seat itself.

In most tackle shops you will find no end of blanks that conform to the basic design as far as length, power and blank/tip con-

27

LINE CLASS	SPECIES OF FISH
12 lbs	Bass, whiting, dogfish, plaice, dabs, common eels, smooth hounds.
20 lbs	Tope, cod, rays, turbot, pollack.
30 lbs	Tope, big cod, ling, big pollack.
50 lbs.	Sharks, halibut, conger.

INCREASE line class one step for dee *water and fast tides which demand heavie* *than normal weights. INCREASE fo* *obstructed marks like wrecks and pinnacl* *rocks unless you are particularly skilfu* *DECREASE line class for extra sport in eas* *waters and open ground.*

The following table shows the two most useful all-round outfits for ground fishing:

LINE CLASS	GENERAL CONDITION
20 lb	Shallow-medium depth water, clean ground, modest tides.
30 lb	Deep water, faster tides, mixed bottom.

It is assumed that you will be fishing on th *drift or from an anchored boat, without cas* *ing away from the hull. (Tackle for uptid* *casting is essentially different as will b* *discussed later.)*

28

Olb line class rods are certainly the most versatile choice for general offshore shing.

he all metal Modalock is the traditional favourite of amateur and professional od builders.

struction are concerned. You will probably need to choose from a shortlist of a dozen, all potentially suitable but different in both finish and price.

Uptide casting

A boat anchored in fast-moving water creates a massive 'V' shaped wake that deters some species of fish. If the water is deep enough to dissipate the commotion, fish will still swim under the shadow of the hull and find your baited tackle.

In shallow water – less than 35-50 ft – the 'V' wake disturbs the seabed to such an extent, that cautious species of fish like cod, bass and rays move out of the immediate area. Shoals swimming with the tide divert upstream of the anchor rope to avoid disturbance. Nothing in the way of groundbaiting or hook bait presentation will prompt them to enter the 'V'.

The logical answer is to cast baits well away from the boat, so that they lie in quiet water. Sometimes ordinary boat tackle does the trick, but not without a struggle. Short rods and heavy reels are brutes to cast even 50 yds. It is a wasted effort anyway: the tackle drifts out of control in the tide.

Special tackle and methods exist to combat the difficulty of casting and bait anchorage. The style of fishing, known as boatcasting, or uptide fishing, is now so well established that it merits equal ranking with conventional fishing. It does not solve all problems associated with boat fishing. Sometimes it is quite out of place; but on the

Plenty of length, action and low-down power as key ingredients in uptide rod blanks.

50lb Essex Tope boated by John Sait (left) from Alf Barnard's 'Boy Carl' 35 miles offshore.

ight ground in the cod, bass and ray sea-ons especially, it takes five fish to every ne hooked under the hull on conventional ear.

The pioneers of uptide fishing either xtended their ordinary boat rods by nserting a longer butt section, or they took long a standard beach casting rod. Finding he beach rod a bit too long and clumsy for oating, they cut down the handle. ventually, uptide rods evolved as a 9–11 ft lank kitted out with standard beach rings nd fittings.

Line class numbers are dropped in favour f casting weight classifications. All kinds of ptide rods are available in kit form and art-built. The vast majority fall into either he 4 oz or 6 oz casting weight range. You eed two basic rods to cover a full year's

fishing, which essentially will be for bass and rays in spring and summer, for cod and whiting bashing in winter. Summer tides and calm seas allow considerable leeway in sinker weight and rod power. Some anglers go down to 1 oz sinkers on carp rods. Most standardise on the 4 oz rod, which is usually capable of handling between 2 and 5 ozs.

Heavier tackle is necessary in winter, not so much because of the size and power of fish – though of course a 20 lb cod is quite a handful – but because the water is rougher and the tides are much more powerful. 6 ozs is about right for general uptide casting, yet the rod still needs enough backbone to lob out 8 ozs on the big spring tides.

The first rod you build should be chosen according to season and species. Local anglers and skippers can put you right on that score, then it is a question of finding a suitable blank in the tackle shop. And that is where you could run into trouble. In some areas of the country uptide fishing is in its infancy. You should visit a specialist dealer like Rod and Line, Lewisham; Breakaway Tackle of Ipswich; Simpson's of Turnford; or Don's of Edmonton. Most of these specialists offer an excellent mail order service, too. Bare blanks and kits of all kinds are readily available.

General features of an uptide rod

Average length is about 9½ ft. Fibreglass blanks are very popular and conform to the fast-taper design which casts smoothly and powerfully with the short flick necessary from a crowded boat. Most rods comprise a tip section about 6 ft long which is spigot jointed to a butt, either of plain fibreglass or with a section of aluminium alloy tube between reel seat and butt cap. Check that the spigot seats deeply into the tip and that the joint is well reinforced with whipping threads. Uptide rod spigots take a beating and risk splitting the blank under full load. Some of the more conscientious rod builders add a band of brass to the base of the female joint as extra insurance. It is probably unnecessary, but certainly does no harm.

Reel seats, handle grips and rings are exactly the same as those fitted to beach casting rods. Choose Fuji-type, Seymo or Dynaflo rings in preference to plain wire. The FPS reel seat is far tougher than a snap-lock or a pair of hose clips. Where weight of rod doesn't bother you, aim for the chromed brass winch fitting. You can depend on it for long service life on the heavier casting rods which toss 6–8 oz leads.

Specialist boat rods

Spinning, trolling and game-fishing blanks are available for that limited number of rod builders who expand their horizons beyond ordinary boat fishing and uptide casting. In time you may develop an interest of your own. At the moment it is better to steer clear of anything out of the ordinary, particularly if it means shelling out unnecessary cash. Worse, you may be persuaded to buy specialist tackle to use for standard techniques.

It is unlikely that you will end up with too light a rod – one aimed at the spinning market, say. Newcomers usually have preconceived ideas about the size and power of sea fishes, and if anything they tend to go for super-heavy gear. It is all too easy to talk yourself into buying the strongest blank in the shop.

50 lb class tackle itself outguns most species of British fish, but there are plenty of anglers who insist on 80 lb class rods capable of landing Jaws. Steer clear of this type of equipment until you have assessed its real worth. If you eventually take up halibut fishing or the like, super-tackle may be the answer. Keep your money in your pocket until you know the score. The rules for now are simple. Ask before you buy; stick to ordinary line class rods or uptide casters.

Beach fishing rods

Without a doubt, casting a bait a long way is the most dominant skill in successful beach and surf angling. That being so, blank selection is critically important. Rod design has evolved to the stage where super casting blanks are produced by a number of top manufacturers. Beware of outdated

Light tackle adds enormously to the fun of boat fishing.

designs and inferior quality products that are also available. Cheap does not always mean inferior, but particularly in this game you usually get exactly what you pay for.

A good beach rod must do more than cast. If casting were the only consideration, everyone would use rods identical to the current tournament monsters that throw 5¼ oz sinkers over 275 yds. However, such beasts are impossible for the average beach angler to handle, and they have little practical application to everyday beach work.

An 11–13 ft fishing blank of medium-fast action is a much better investment. Exact length will vary somewhat depending on your height, strength and casting style. 11½–12 ft is an excellent starting point for experiment. Owing to the lightness and smooth-casting characteristics of the latest blank materials, a change from old glassfibre to composite or carbonfibre may permit an extra foot on the tip.

Unlike freshwater fishermen, beach enthusiasts need not choose special rods for various species and fishing conditions. Versatility is the target: look for one rod – or an identical pair – capable of tackling calm and rough water, mastering a reasonable span of light-to-heavy tackle; sensitive enough for dabs, yet with enough backbone in reserve to battle heavy swells and specimen cod. Tip flexibility and low-down power are essential design features. Blank action should be forgiving enough to compensate for rough casting and to avoid snapping light lines.

Rods of that all-round ability were once a pipedream, but modern designs come close to perfection. The ideal blank for pendulum casting has a rigid or semi-rigid butt, progressive middle and upper shaft that shoots the tackle away at top speed, and a finely tapered tip for smoothing delivery and to

iron out multiplier reel backlash. According to manufacturer's individual whims, such blanks are termed medium-fast or fast.

Most high-performance surf rods are constructed from a short handle plus a separate tip, usually between 7¾ and 8½ f long. Most anglers prefer the one-piece tip since it is a little cheaper and, theoretically should be tougher and of better action However, there are some good two equal-length section rods available for anglers who cannot carry and store those long, inconvenient tips.

Choice of tip material depends on how much you want to spend, and how important you rate casting performance and fishing sensitivity. Beginners are better off with plain glassfibre. Cash outlay is low, and such blanks are middle-of-the-road in performance and in their demands on the angler himself. Fibreglass takes a lot of abuse and is fairly versatile. On the other hand, it is still capable of topping 200 yards, so there's plenty of encouragement to learn good technique. Thousands of experienced beach fishermen never consider looking for anything better.

'S' grade fibreglass is the next step forward in design sophistication. It is lighter, steelier and more sensitive, yet costs nowhere near as much as carbonfibre. The strands of fibre are so tough that breakages are a thing of the past even if the rod is severely abused or grossly overloaded with sinker weight. Unfortunately, good 'S' glass rods are few and far between.

Carbonfibre and carbon/glass laminated tips are unmatched for casting performance and angling finesse. Their smooth, powerful acceleration adds yards to your cast (assuming the technique is good enough), and if sheer distance is the name of the game where you fish, that extra distance may lead to bigger catches. Lying between

The beach fisherman's dilemma: how to balance good casting power against adequate bite sensitivity for small fish.

one half and two-thirds the weight of an equally powerful glass blank, a semi-carbon, or carbon beachmaster is also slimmer, better balanced in hand, and far more sensitive to bites.

Price is the disadvantage. You can buy four glass blanks for the outlay on one carbon. Although cheaper carbon and composite blanks are trickling into the shops, they are pretty poor value. If you want the best, be ready to invest your money in reputable British tackle of proven track record. At the time of writing, there is not one Far Eastern surf blank worth even fleeting consideration.

Every leading surf blank manufacturer offers a range of handles in lengths and materials to match everyone's pocket and performance. Modern rods incorporate a butt of parallel hollow glass, high tensile

duralumin, carbonfibre, glass/carbon laminate or duralumin sheathed with glass or carbonfibre.

Plain glass is forgiving but not very powerful — fine for the beginner and for moderate casting ranges, but not stiff and zippy enough for real power.

Tubular aluminium alloy (duralumin) tubing is about the same weight as glass, yet hardly bends under severe pressure. Its stiffness alone boosts casting power, and makes the material a reasonably good match for all blanks, even carbonfibre. The drawbacks are rapid corrosion, harshness, and no forgiveness of casting and fishing error. Even a coat of glassfibre fails to protect the handle from saltwater — most butts rot from the inside out.

Carbonfibre butts are the best of the lot. Expensive too. But if sheer smoothness,

Surf bass are easy to hook on medium-fast glassfibre blanks. You can build such a rod for less than £40.

Champion surfcaster Neil Mackellow needs an ultra-powerful rod to break tournament records. However, he uses much softer rods for fishing.

11½ft semi-carbon pendulum blanks offer the perfect solution to the demands of modern shore fishing.

ightning response, ultimate casting power and unbeatable balance and general handling are high on your list of priorities, there really is no other choice. Carbonfibre butts are the perfect match for today's semi-carbons, composites like Graphite 'S' and high-content carbon itself.

Sea blank manufacturers

Sea angling is a fast-changing world. Blanks in favour today will be discarded tomorrow. There is no great value, then, in listing models by name and number. A great many specialist tackle shops order blanks designed to their own local requirements, and you will not find those models catalogued by the manufacturer himself. The only way to get the right sea blank is to go to a well-respected dealer like those mentioned in the uptide section, and either take his advice or pick out a blank which matches your preconceived ideas on length, action and power.

Most experts would not be seen dead with anything but British. Zziplex carbons are the standard by which all surfcasting and uptide blanks are judged.

BASIC BUILDING MATERIALS AND TECHNIQUES

HANDLES

Cork

Until recently cork has always been considered the most suitable material for making a full length rod handle. Cork is light, waterproof, easily shaped and repaired, comfortable to hold and reasonably priced. It looks good and somehow feels just right. In the case of a float rod which is usually held throughout a fishing session, comfort and feel are very important considerations. Cork also has perfect resilience, so that when the reel is slotted into its fittings the material compresses to a good tight fit.

The best handles are made with broad ring corks which come in various sizes and diameters matched to different types of rods. The smallest are used for fly rods, medium for coarse rods and the big ones for beach and boat saltwater tackle.

The first step in making a cork handle is roughly to match a set of bored corks to the length and diameter of the blank's butt. With a predetermined idea of how you want the handle to be (more on this later) it is simple to test-fit corks on to the blank by trial and error until you build up the necessary length. If the blank is parallel throughout the butt area, all corks can be the same size. Check them just the same. With a tapered butt it is even more important to test beforehand because the central hole of graded corks must grade downward with falling blank diameter.

Make sure the corks fit snugly. It is seldom possible to get a perfect fit, in which case aim for overtight rather than loose. Tight fitting corks are soon enlarged with a round file or abrasive paper but oversize corks never can be glued properly and result in a weak spot on the handle. Corks that are slightly too tight slide into position if you twist them carefully down the blank, but do split or crack occasionally. Buy a few spares with a small hole just in case; they can be enlarged to fit anywhere on the handle.

Apart from being available individually, bored corks are sold in sections several inches long. Although the bored hole is parallel, the section is still short enough to be adapted to a tapered blank. In any case, the hole can be enlarged as described. Whatever the case, preformed cork sections certainly hasten rod construction.

Buy only good quality corks. Poor cork is characterised by deep pits and cracks which not only spell weakness (they split under modest pressure) but is also very difficult to cut to shape and to finish smoothly.

It is rarely the dealer's fault that his cork stocks are poor. The market fluctuates; sometimes a whole batch is excellent, yet the next consignment is rubbish. Shopping around is the answer.

Having tested the corks on the butt, number them from top to bottom before pulling them off the blank. Now they can be glued on in the same sequence, which ensures a perfect match.

Opinions differ on the choice of glue for cork handles. Some builders prefer Araldite, but I don't like it because it sets rock hard and makes rubbing down and shaping too laborious. Others swear by Bostik or household glue, and some professionals use nothing but Cascamite. I use Evostik Resin W woodworking glue (not contact adhesive) which comes in convenient nozzled containers. Being ready mixed and creamy, Resin W is easy and clean to work with, sets semi-hard, and is quickly filed and sanded. However, it takes longer to set than other glues and must stand for 24 hours before cork shaping begins.

If you know a professional lathe operator, ask him to turn your handle to the right diameter and shape. Failing that, hand shaping is relatively simple provided you take your time and work carefully. All you need is a coarse file; some coarse, medium, and fine sandpaper; and a pencil.

One of the pleasures of making your own

Tools and basic materials for amateur rod building.

Best quality rod corks are the only kind worth buying.

With care and skill, you can make the whole rod with these simple tools.

handle is that it can be shaped exactly how you fancy. The photographs show examples of profiles for full-length cork handles which look good and prevent the reel fittings from sliding off the end of the rod. Remember that reel fittings must be slid on to the main section of the handle before you finish the bottom. Leave the bottom three corks until the rest of the butt is complete, then slide on your reel fittings, glue those extra sections into place and shape them to blend in with the corks above.

Plastic butt caps are an alternative to cork ends. This way you can glue and shape all the corks at once. Plastic never looks as neat as shaped cork but does save time and is highly practical in as much as it protects the butt and prevents reel fittings falling off. Most plastic caps weigh virtually nothing

and have no affect on the rod's handling or balance.

Handle length and diameter are a personal choice, but thin handles are more comfortable and less tiring to hold for hours on end. They are the best option for float and fly rods. Low diameter carbon blanks can support very slim cork handles less than an inch in diameter, but fast taper glass blanks may be so thick that you have little choice in handle specification. Some very fast tapered rods incorporate a separate parallel butt section that glues inside the main blank, in which case you should be able to fit comfortably slim corks.

Avoid those excessively long full-cork handles seen on some mass produced freshwater rods. It is a mystery why some manufacturers and even custom builders till insist on supplying them. What happens is that at the design stage a blank is rolled on too short a mandrel, then is stretched to the required length by an overlong butt extension. The resulting overlap joint is hidden under a cork handle some 30 ins long. Most handles this long are awkward, unbalanced, and hamper good tackle control. If you purchase a kit, make sure it does not feature such blank and handle construction. Even if you shortened the handle, the finished rod would still be out of balance and unnecessarily weak.

A freshwater rod handle should rarely be longer than 25 ins. Mine are 23 ins, which suits me personally. A reliable method of finding your own handle length is to hold the rod at arms length in front of you with the extreme end of the butt tucked under your armpit. Handle length should be about where the centre of your palm grips the blank. Alternatively, hold the as yet unfinished corks at the point where the reel will sit, and tuck the handle under your forearm. Only 4–5 ins of cork should extend past your elbow.

Now to fit and shape the handle. Begin by lightly sanding the butt with coarse sandpaper to provide good glue adhesion. Apply glue to the bottom of the butt and slide the first of the corks (which have already been numbered) over the glued patch. Give each cork a couple of twists to spread the glue evenly. Do not forget to leave off the three final corks if your prefer a shaped butt rather than a plastic cap.

Wipe away any glue that oozed from behind the cork rings, and re-spread it on the

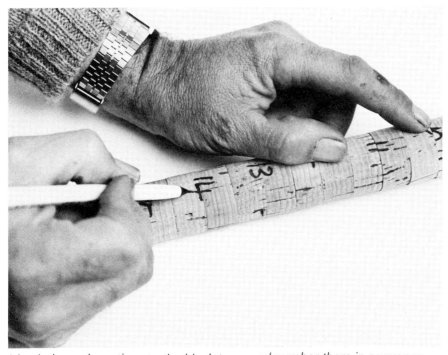

Match the cork sections to the blank taper and number them in sequence.

blank where the next ring fits. Top up with extra glue if necessary, slide on the next ring . . . and so on. Apply a little glue to the inner cheeks of each ring so that they stick to each other as well as to the blank. Clean off excess glue as you progress up the handle, and finally put the butt aside until the glue is absolutely hardened.

Before shaping the corks, wrap a few turns of masking tape or Sellotape around the blank immediately above the handle to protect its surface from accidental abrasion by file and sandpaper. Begin shaping by marking straight lines down the handle with a felt pen or pencil, each line about $\frac{3}{4}$ in apart around the cork's circumference. Now, using a coarse file, begin cutting back the corks with long, even strokes that flow down the handle and slightly across. Work

along each line in turn. Carefully avoid taking too much material from the up-rod end of the corks where you will eventually form a handle bulge. Leave on plenty of cork for later.

Continue to cut away until you are left with a roughly polygonal shape. File away each corner of the cross-section until the handle assumes its correct rounded shape. If the handle is still too thick, mark a new set of lines and repeat the process until diameter falls within $\frac{1}{4}$ in of your preference.

Lay the file aside and start working with coarse sandpaper. Shape and smooth the corks until the handle is straight and even. Check diameter with calipers, and test-fit the reel clamps on the lower corks. As the handle falls closer and closer to its correct diameter, change to medium paper. Work

Simple test for correct handle length.

Gluing cork into position.

Filing the corks into rough shape.

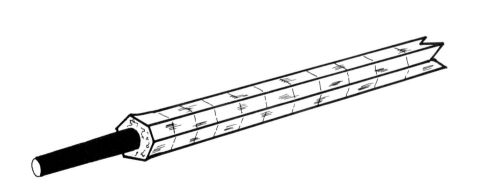

PRELIMINARY HEXAGONAL SHAPE TO CORK HANDLE

43

Reducing diameter with coarse sandpaper.

Fitting the collars.

n, and regularly check the reel fittings on the handle. When they *just* slide on, stop cutting.

Which shape to form at the top and bottom of the handle is a matter of choice. I usually make a bell shape or cone at the top, and a rounded profile at the bottom. Shaping is a freehand exercise with coarse sandpaper wrapped around a dowel or pencil.

Now use fine sandpaper to obtain a really smooth professional finish. If you have used good quality corks, you will be surprised to find that your handle looks every bit as good as those on factory rods. However, even the best corks hold a few minor surface imperfections. Mix some fine cork dust and adhesive into a smooth paste, and smear it into any flaw. When the filler dries, polish off the residue with fine paper.

Reel fittings should now slide freely but retain a good snug fit. Too loose, and they will never stop the reel working free and twisting on the handle. If you use a plastic butt cap, now is the time to put it on. There is no need for glue if you have a tight fit, which is easily obtained by dousing the cap in hot water for a minute to make the plastic more pliable. On cooling, the cap contracts tightly on to the handle end. If you prefer shaped corks instead of a cap, the final sections should now be glued into place and sanded to match the rest of the handle.

Preshaped cork handles come in pieces which are slid over the blank butt and glued into position. Since the corks are already sanded and finished, and the tops and bottoms pre-shaped, here is a convenient,

Carving the handle end.

45

rapid way to produce a serviceable handle with minimum effort. Trouble is, quickness and convenience are paid for in quality. The handle's fit on to the blank is never as good as it is with individually chosen cork rings. Manufacturers use cheap materials to make the sections and each ring of cork is filled and sanded to help hide substantial imperfections.

Other handle materials

Several synthetic handle materials are now available, Duplon proving a real challenge to the traditional superiority of corks. It is already available in preshaped sections for freshwater rods and with taper-bored sections for blanks of tapering wall.

Duplon is simple to fit. Just apply adhesive to the blank and slide the pre shaped sections into position. Being black it looks good; and its firm velvety texture feels nice in hand. It cannot be shaped – but that is hardly necessary since the hard work has already been done for you by the manufacturer. Unfortunately because it is softer than cork, its grip on the reel is not quite as secure. Nevertheless, it is a useful material used more and more often on factory built rods, and eventually it may replace cork.

Normark supply Orblon handle material which can be shaped by the angler. It is a high density foam-rubbery black sleeve supplied in maximum lengths of 6 ft. Tackle dealers cut it into appropriate pieces for rod making. Various diameters are available

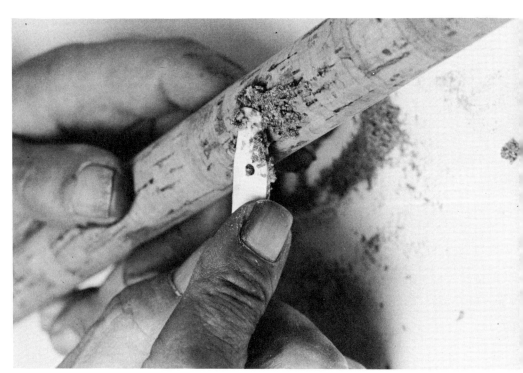

Filling the handle with a paste of glue and cork dust.

Plastic and aluminium sliding collars for cork handles.

from 30–42 mm, and with central holes ranging from 8–26 mm in 2 mm increments.

Orblon files down, sands and finishes into trendy black grip which, like cork, is twisted on to the blank and glued down. Because it is denser than Duplon, the Normark product provides better reel security.

Reel fittings for full length handles

Plain sliding collars are the most popular reel fittings for full length rod handles. They are made from various materials like plain aluminium, black anodised aluminium and plastic, all of them notoriously unreliable since they work loose on the reel stand. One minute you are fishing happily, the next scrabbling in mud or ten feet of water trying to recover a reel which suddenly dropped off the rod handle. The only sliding collars I can recommend are John Roberts Reelfits, of moulded tough black nylon and shaped to blend with the reel foot. Reelfits, and for that matter any of the sliding cone collars, must be a snug fit on the handle itself. Reelfits are available in three diameters only: 22 mm, 23.5 mm, and 25 mm.

Abbreviated handles for carp, pike and sea rods

There is no reason why you cannot make a full length handle for any of these rods.

Many anglers do just that on their carp and pike rods, but it is rare to see a modern beach blank thus built. Today's preference is towards an abbreviated handle with three short grips. Only two grips are necessary on pike and carp rods – one at the extreme butt, one just below the reel seat. Beach and boat rods sport an extra grip above the reel seat because, unlike freshwater men, sea anglers hold the rod above the reel position for better control and stronger leverage. The third grip makes life a lot easier when you pump in heavy sinkers or use finger and thumb to guide line back on to a multiplier reel.

Bored cork rings, preshaped corks or Duplon/Orblon can be used for abbreviated handles; additionally, plastic mouldings and various plain rubber grips are available in the tackle shops. Some anglers are happy to f[it] motorbike or lawnmower handle bar grip[s]. Fit all these handles by smearing glue on th[e] appropriate section of blank and sliding th[e] grip into place. Shape Orblon as you would [a] section of cork. Plastic or rubber end cap[s] finish the job.

You will need to glue on a screw o[r] clamp-type reel fitting. Choose a reel sea[t] that matches the grips. Together they form [a] unit which either compliments the blank o[r] destroys its feel. Note: before gluing an[y] fixed reel seat, be sure it aligns with the sid[e] of the blank which will eventually suppo[rt] the rings. Also, see notes on spin[e] determination.

Fuji Snaplocks are the simplest type o[f] reel seat. They grip reels with a zip-up clam[p] which locks the reel stand against the blan[k].

The simplest handle of all – just a reel seat glued to the bare blank.

Synthetic abbreviated grips are popular in freshwater and sea angling.

Comfortable handles are a blessing in cold weather. Len Head unhooks a December chub.

A Fuji snaplock taped to cork strip on a light beachcasting blank.

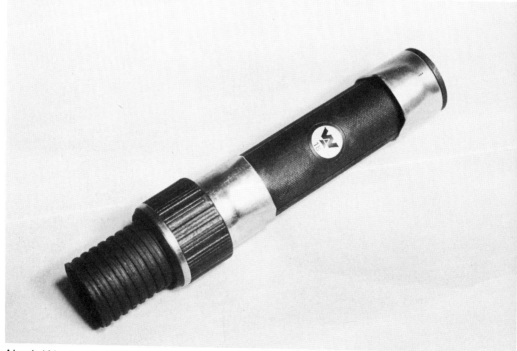

North Western's WFRS tubular reel seat is a British copy of a Japanese product!

A Snaplock can either be glued directly to the blank or attached on top of the grip material. Whip-on and tubular framed versions are available. They are cheap and easy to fit but do not look very neat; and although the reel seldom actually drops off the rod, Snaplocks tend to rock sideways under pressure. This fault can be cured or at least reduced by whipping the seat to an underlay of rubber cut from a tyre inner tube.

Fuji Connespin tube fittings are almost as simple to attach. The Connespin is a moulded PVC top handle grip which incorporates a zip-up clasp reel fitting similar to a Snaplock. You just glue it into place. It is available in one size only, 16.5 mm bore. Slim blanks can be built up in diameter by spiral wraps of thread well saturated with adhesive.

Excellent screw fittings are available in the Fuji FPS range, with bore diameters between 18 and 32 mm in 2 mm increments. There are two versions: one moulded from plastic/glass composite, the other of carbon and glass. The latter is ultra light and thus specially suited to lightweight carbonfibre blanks.

Equally good are the new British fittings which look similar to the FPS. Bore sizes are 18–28 mm; the body is a very light carbon-based plastic moulding and the clamps are of stainless steel. The fitting is actually cheaper than its Japanese counterpart. North Western Blanks distribute the seat under reference WFRS.

Match the bore of the fitting to the diameter of the blank where it is to be glued. Fit to a 3 in foregrip (optional) and 5 in lower

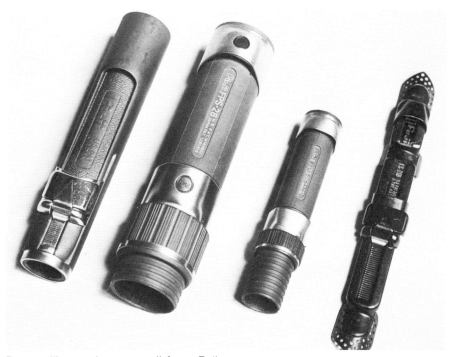

Best selling reel seats – all from Fuji.

51

grip on pike and carp rods. Black Duplon or Orblon looks good fitted this way, especially on carbonfibre blanks. The butt grip should also match the reel seat.

To avoid problems, assemble the abbreviated handle in sequence. Start with the butt grip which must be slid *down* the blank from the spigot end, and glue it into position with just enough space left for the butt cap. Most blanks can be married to a grip of just the right bore for a perfect fit. Next, slide on and glue down the lower reel grip. Cement the reel seat into place (checking alignment with ring's position), then press on the upper reel grip. Upper grips should butt tightly against the ends of the seat.

Abbreviated handles for sea rods are made the same way but the upper foregrip is lengthened to 6–7 ins. Orblon and cork are better than Duplon which is a little too spongy to give the firm grip necessary for powerful fishing.

Use the light, corrosion-proof FPS or British WFRS reel fittings which have bore sizes adequate for most sea blanks. You don't want heavy fittings that add surplus weight; and it makes no sense to fit accessories that rot in a few months.

Fuji Snaplocks are certainly inferior to screw fittings because they fail to provide a solid anchorage for the reel, especially a big surfcasting fixed spool. There is nothing more annoying than a reel that waggles about in its seat while you try to coax a heavy fish to shore or boat.

All beach and boat rods need comfortable, soft butt caps due to the pressure exerted on the angler's stomach or groin while he retrieves line under pressure. Soft caps also protect the angler's chest from injury should the sinker snap in mid cast and the rod butt slam into his body. Various rubber or plastic butt caps are available; many keen fishermen choose a rubber pad designed for the tips of walking sticks and crutches. Its broad, stippled base is a stable and durable anchoring point for propping the rod butt in sand, shingle and against smooth concrete.

You don't have to use hand grips at all. The butt can be left bare and the reel attached by a pair of hosepipe clips. Such rods look primitive but they work very well, and they offer great advantages for the beach angler. Reel position can be changed instantly to match different weights of sinkers and various casting styles.

Handle length and reel position are personal factors which can make a tremendous difference to rod performance and angler comfort. The secret is to match tackle to your physical size and strength. If you choose the barebones handle with just hoseclips to hold the reel there are no problems since you can shift the reel up and down the butt into exactly the right place for hard casting. Placing a fixed reel seat is much more hazardous because once glued it is usually impossible to move without ruining the seat, and perhaps the butt as well. In any case, it means shifting grips – in other words you must rebuild the entire handle.

The most likely reel position for the average beach angler is 29–32 ins from the butt cap. See how that feels by testing the rod with the seat handheld or taped in position. Then go ahead with the glue. Such preliminary tests save a great deal of time and expense and should guarantee spot-on results. Judge by the feel of the rod, how smoothly it casts, and by the distances produced. Boat rods are designed on the same principle, but the preferred reel height is somewhat lower – between 12 and 18 ins for traditional style and 20–25 ins for uptide.

The gap left bare between abbreviated grips or on barebones rods may be covered

Soft rubber caps are a wise safety precaution for heavy surf rods, especially backcasters.

Playing heavy fish from a boat is much more comfortable with a harness belt. Fit the rod handle with the appropriate gimbel.

with various materials such as leather, rubber strip or plastic tape. Most are self adhesive, but a few must be glued to the butt. The two ends have a habit of coming unstuck whatever covering you choose, so it is standard practice to seal them with a broad whipping.

Shrink tube sleeves are an alternative. Shrink tube – black, blue, red, and clear are the most widely available colours – is a heat sensitive plastic that tightens on to the blank under moderate heat. It is better applied before grips and reel seat are glued down. Slide a slightly overlong sleeve on to the butt and shrink it tight by pouring on boiling water. Or use carefully controlled heat from a gas ring or electric fire. The tube shrinks to a neat, close fit and all that remains is to trim the ends. In the case of aluminium beach rod

butts, roll excess plastic inside the butt end, then jam on the butt cap. This helps prevent saltwater creeping into the rod and eating away at the aluminium walls.

Fly rod handles and fittings

A thin scroll shape is probably the most comfortable grip for a trout rod handle. It need not be longer than 7 or 8 inches for singlehanded casting. Preshaped complete handles in cork and Duplon are available from good tackle shops. Just glue them into place. Duplon is particularly comfortable. Alternatively, shape your own grip from cork rings or Orblon tube.

A confusing array of trout reel fittings is available, ranging from super quality pewter

Shrink tube and hoseclips are an excellent choice for long range surfcasting. The reel can be positioned exactly according to physique and personal preference.

nd bronze anodised aluminium to cheap nd nasty plastics. Choose a lightweight, igh quality fitting with reliable screw lock lamps that grip the reel tightly. Trout fly eels also have the habit of working loose nd falling off the rod.

I dislike the popular fitting with a fixed reel lasp on one end to take the reel foot, and a lual screw/clasp on the other end. Avoid hem because they don't provide a atisfactory fit unless you screw down the ollars so tightly that they freeze on the hreads. Unfortunately, most otherwise jood fittings are made the wrong way around – they clamp the reel to the extreme end of the butt, where it clogs with mud and jrit when the rod is laid down. A more sensible design would clamp the reel nearer the handle corks and allow a couple of inches clearance below for resting the rod.

However, several trout fittings are available with reversible end buttons which fit either way up. One is the Fuji FPS plastic/glass seat; another the Hopkins & Holloway AP/154, in pewter or bronze aluminium alloy. The same company produces a black anodised reel seat, ref. 4A/154. All are available in small bores to match carbonfibre and boron blanks.

RINGS AND WHIPPINGS

Ring design has kept pace with rod blank development. Home builders choose from a variety of lightweight, hardwearing, low friction rings by Fuji, Hopkins & Holloway, and Daiwa. Fuji were first to market a ring incorporating a one piece wire frame, an

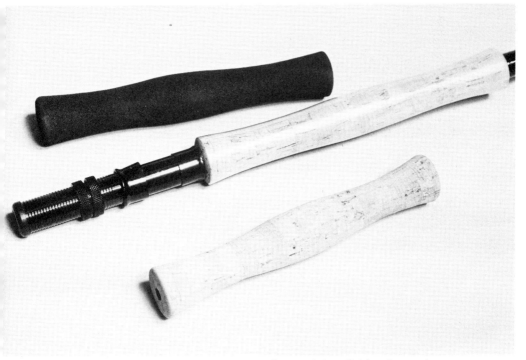

Cork and Orblon fly rod handles. They are equally good, but Orblon is much easier to fit.

Fuji FPS and Hopkins & Holloway fly rod seats. Fuji use plastic, whereas the British company manufacture in aluminium.

outer shock absorber to smooth line travel, and a special hard inner ring of aluminium oxide that minimises friction and damage to both ring and fishing line.

Their new SiC (silicon carbide) liner is even tougher. The inner ring is diamond polished to minimise friction, and is claimed to be 12 times as hard as stainless steel. Equally good British made rings from Hopkins & Holloway — the Seymo range — offer the same one-piece frame with liners of titania/alumina oxide. Concave frame feet provide stability on the blank, and the rings are very light indeed. Hopkins & Holloway also market a more economical Dialite model, which uses an inner ring of hardchrome claimed to compare favourably with expensive ceramic liners.

Daiwa's Dynaflo is the fourth option. Here the inner ring is crafted from low friction toughened stainless steel. Some rod makers consider Dynaflos to be the strongest rings of all, and thus a particularly wise choice for hard working rods like beachcasters. However, there is a shortage of supplies at the moment with Daiwa apparently using stocks on their own range of rods.

In my experience Fujis and Seymos are just as good provided you choose the correct pattern for the rod. Fuji's range of rings is larger, but Hopkins & Holloway are catching up fast. The new Fuji SiCs do appear to reduce friction, though it is unlikely they make a significant — or even measurable — difference to casting range. Perhaps they are justified on expensive custom made rods . . . but be ready to dig deep into your wallet.

Indeed, all these one piece framed rings are relatively expensive, costing up to twice as much as chromed wire rings. Less line wear, lower friction, and far longer service life certainly justify the higher outlay; in fact, replacement of broken and worn out rings seems to be a thing of the past. One Fuji-ringed float rod I have fished hard for five years still shows not the slightest signs of ring wear.

Certainly if you have invested in a carbonfibre blank it is not worth spoiling the project for the sake of saving a few pounds by whipping on cheap rings. Fit the best; the outlay will guarantee years of reliability and high performance.

Cheap wire rings often have lumps and sharp angles where the pieces have been welded together, and although they do most of the things a ring is supposed to do, they are notoriously unreliable and will break at the joints from the slightest jolt. Damage is usually discovered on the bankside when it is too late to do much about it. Wire rings are very soft, grooving quickly under the attack of nylon lines. They have nothing to recommend them on today's rods.

However, not all wire rings are useless. Hopkins & Holloway manufacture an excellent range of chromed wire rings suitable for most kinds of rods. They are economically priced as well. Basically there are three kinds of chrome rings: bright chrome, hardchrome and black chrome. Hardchrome is about four times harder than bright chrome, and is really the better of the two as a ring making material. For serious

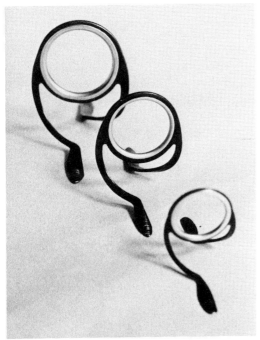

Hopkins & Holloway Dialite rings.

Daiwa Dynaflo (top) and Fuji aluminium oxide rings.

rod building, look no farther.

Black chromed rings are a joke, surely? The ring centre lasts barely one season before grooving deeply. In order to pander to the current rage for everything in angling to be coloured black, ring makers would eventually have had to introduce black chrome, but here is a classic case of marketing forces taking over from practicality. Do not put black chromed rings on your rod unless you plan a complete rebuild after a few months.

If the cost of one-piece frame rings puts you off, why not compromise with a mixture? Use Fuji or Seymo at tip and butt (the rings that take most of the punishment) and fill in with Dialite or hardchromed wire. The system works well on fly, coarse and beach rods, and just about copes with light/medium boat work.

When choosing rings in the tackle shop, inspect each one carefully. Reject any that appear lopsided or out of shape, those with insecure or sharp-edged welds where wire frames have been jointed, and all rings without perfectly smooth centres for perfect line travel. A small magnifying glass is a useful aid to checking ring centres and the frames of tiny freshwater and fly models.

Ring quality depends on how much you are willing to pay. Sizes, spacings and numbers reflect the type and action of rod you aim to build. Float rods used for fine line fishing need enough high-standing rings to carry the line along the full curve of the blank. Use the least number to achieve a perfect match; as light as modern rings are, they still add unnecessary weight which alters blank response and performance. More rings are positioned towards the blank tip than at the butt where the bend is less pronounced. Ample rings also minimise line bowing in the wind; and high-standing models prevent line sticking to the blank in rain or damp conditions.

A light, flexible ring moves with the blank as it bends. Fitting heavy, wide braced, rigid rings to a light float rod would stiffen the action and ruin its performance, and will also make it feel heavy and unbalanced in hand.

Probably best for float rods are Fuji BMVFG match guides – three legged, narrow profile rings of flexible, one-piece construction. Choose a tip ring that allows a straight flow of line from the preceding intermediate. The Fuji BMVFT is an excellent match, but you could use a lighter fly rod model Fuji BFT which is preferred by many professional builders. Appropriate silicon carbide match ring combinations are MVSG and MVST.

Alternatively, fit Seymo GHI/B/2 butt and intermediate rings matched to the THI/C/2 tip or the fly ring THI/B. The new Hopkins and Holloway Dialite series are equally impressive, giving high quality coupled to attractive prices. Try match rod intermediates GHCD and the appropriate THCD/2 tip ring.

Ringing leger rods

Leger rods are generally used with higher breaking strain lines and heavier leads. Since line is usually held tight between the lead and rod tip, swingtip, or butt indicator, line bowing/sticking problems found on match tackle are rarely encountered. You therefore need fewer rings, and there is less need for high stand-off frames.

However, it is necessary to submerge the rod tip in this style of fishing, and this results in line sticking to the tip and reducing bite sensitivity. Tightening line to the indicator or rod top usually unsticks the nylon, but it can remain adhered and unnoticed. That little bit of extra friction might be enough to make a

Fuji BMVG rings.

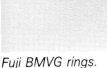

Hopkins & Holloway Seymo GH1/B.

fish drop the bait. For that reason I believe leger rod rings should be high standing *if* they are strong enough. Line stick on sunk rod tips is particularly common on leger rods used with light lines and quiver tips.

Convention says that heavy wire, tough rod rings must be fitted to leger rods. This is true enough for rods used for heavy work such as feeder fishing for big tench, bream and barbel, or to battle hard fighting carp and pike. In my opinion though, light rings like Fuji BMVFG recommended for float rods would be equally well suited for light leger rods. You will enjoy the definite advantages of better flexibility, enhanced tackle control and lighter weight.

If you intend using detachable quiver, spring or swing tips, choose a threaded tip ring for instant indicator attachment. The standard tip ring matched to Fuji BMVFG is either S-BMRFT, or the silicon carbide S-MVST.

Rods with spliced quivers are extremely thin at the tip, so that whipping on standard rings becomes impractical. Special quiver mini-rings are available, again in the Fuji range: single leg BMKFG intermediates and BMKFT tip, both of them low friction aluminium oxide lined. These rings also match up with standard BMVFG intermediates and are made in four sizes to enable gradual reduction in ring diameter towards the tip.

Hopkins & Holloway produce a special wire midget guide for quivers: 986 intermediates and 996 tip. The wire tip ring is prone to causing line to grate alarmingly when the rod is bent against a fish, so the ring really cannot be recommended despite its low cost. In any case, superior Fuji quiver tip rings are surprisingly inexpensive and must be considered the only sensible choice to match high quality rings on the rest of the blank. Make sure you whip on enough mini-rings to follow the delicate curve of the quiver.

Long range rods for barbel, bream and big tench require a slightly sturdier ring for the heavier fishing techniques involved. Yet it is still important to aim for the lightest rings possible, and again it pays to use a reasonably high standing model. They are less important on these rods, but are no disadvantage either.

If your bank balance runs to it, silicon carbide SVSG/HVSG rings would be hard to beat. The wire frame is strong for its weight; the three-legged, narrow profile frame flexes nicely with the blank.

Seymo high stand-off match guide GHI/B/2 is a wider braced, sturdier ring than the Fuji equivalent and would be tough enough for slightly heavier legering. It costs much less than the Fuji. There are only three sizes, but they are adequate if you use the largest for the butt, middle size for the first intermediate, and the smallest for the rest of the intermediates. Matching tip rings are THI/C/2 or the threaded THI/C/3ST for detachable indicators.

Ringing pike and carp rods

These rods come in for rather more strain and heavy work than rods mentioned so far. Rings must be chosen for strength as well as for flexibility, light weight and smooth, low friction centres. Long range carp and pike rods used with shock leaders benefit from rings with wide centres which allow the knot joining leader to main line to glide

through for easy casting. It is possible for a leader knot to rip off light wire narrow centred rings as line hurtles from the spool during a powerful cast.

A strong ring with a reasonably large centre takes this kind of abuse, and provided it is of narrow profile will still flex under the bend of the blank. Over-heavy, widely braced cradle rings sometimes recommended for carp and pike blanks add unnecessary weight and deaden the blank's action because they do not flex with it.

These days, pike and carp rods are used 95 per cent of the time in conjunction with antenna or sensor wheel electronic bite indicators. Although bowing and line stick are not really a problem, reasonably high stand off rings do help the line to slot inside the indicator. Low set rings do not hold the line far enough out from the blank to meet the sensor, an annoying problem with Optonics heads in particular. Provided reasonably high rings are whipped on, the problem is lessened by setting the rod in its test so that the highest rings – butt and first intermediate – are close to the indicator box.

If you are satisfied with nothing but perfect rings, choose SVSG/HVSG silicon carbides from Fuji. Three-legged, fairly high standing, narrow profile, light and tough, they are excellent for this kind of fishing.

On all long range rods, go for biggish butt rings of around 30 mm diameter, and graduate down through the intermediates so as to avoid any sudden steps or angles in the line path. Tips rings are subject to most friction, and are important on rods for heavy hard fighting species like carp and pike. Some rings allow so much friction to build that the line grates when the rod assumes its full power curve. Tackle sometimes threatens to lock solid. Low friction, top quality tips are essential. Ideally, fit silicon carbon Fuji PST.

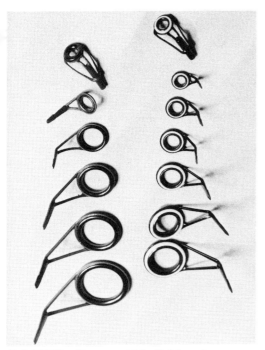

Fuji SPSG silicon carbide (left) and BSPHG aluminium oxide rings for freshwater and light sea fishing.

Single leap are very secure. Even a strip of adhesive tape holds them tightly to the blank.

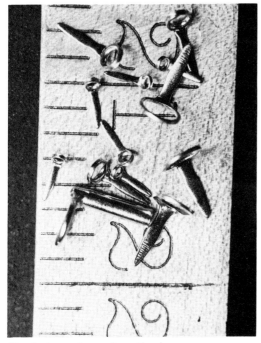

Single leg wire quiver tip rings.

Seymo GH1/C (left) and Fuji BFG fly rod rings.

Fuji BSPHG single-leg guides are popular with carp anglers. They are extremely light; the single foot gives exceptionally good flex with rod action; they are available in graded sizes up to 30 mm so that large butts and intermediates can be used to assist line slotting into indicators and to permit free flow of leader knots.

The single retaining whipping seems too weak for long range work and leader knots, but I know of no problems so far. Another good pattern is the Seymo GHI/E, which has the best flexibility of all. Two bracing feet straddle the blank to ensure firm whipping and a smooth blending with blank action. Daiwa Dynaflos are good carp and pike rings if you can find a supply. So are Fuji BSHG and BNHG, and Hopkins & Holloway Dialites with hardchromed centres. Ordinary welded frame wire rings are inadequate for this style of fishing.

Ringing fly rods

Perhaps more than any other, fly rods need rings that are light and flexible. The lightest, most flexible you can buy are simple snake rings. They are cheap as well. In use though, snakes allow too much line friction and slap against the rod in mid-cast. They are especially bad for shooting a long line. A better and almost equally flexible pattern would be a doubled wire ring. At one time ABU used such designs on a few of their rods, but the ring is no longer available. Fuji and Seymo again hold the key, with single leg fly patterns BFG and GHI/C. Matching tips rings are BFT and THI/B.

Ringing sea rods

Strength of frame and long term durability are most important here. Besides the stress from heavy sinkers and severe fishing con-ditions, sea rings must contend with accidental knocks. I should think there is not one angler who has not dropped his rod on the shingle or had it pulled off the rest by tide and biting fish. Light rings cannot withstand one clout against hard beach or boat gunwhales.

Strong 40–50 lb shock leaders produce relatively bulky leader knots which spell disaster for light wire rings. Abrasive sand and grit picked up by the line and sawn back and forth across the ring soon rips through light metal. Not long ago, regular ring replacement was part and parcel of beach fishing. Today it should no longer be a problem: rings with hard liners should last for years. Popular patterns are Fuji BNHG and BSHG, plus the silicon carbide equivalents NSG. Lighter blanks for bass and flatties could be ringed with Hopkins & Holloway Seymo and Dialite GHCD. Carefully fished, they are useful on heavier tackle as well.

Tip rings receive most of the hard work involved in sea fishing. Insert centred rings are hard wearing but are prone to pop apart under load, especially if the leader knot pings against the liner either on the cast or when a big fish comes ashore. Diamite tips have no insert and are thus recommended for all rods regardless of which rings are chosen for the intermediates and butt. Use a reasonably large ring – say 16 mm.

Tungsten carbide and Carbaloy tip rings are a useful alternative for general boat rods and are indispensible for fishing with wire line. Running wire cuts through most liners except the above mentioned pair, rollers or SiC Fuji. Only the finest brands of roller ring will stand up to long-term duty; and because rollers are heavy and expensive as well, they probably hold little interest and no real advantage for the majority of home rod builders. Indeed, roller rings are of limited value even on heavy trolling and deep water rods.

As Dacron and other braided lines fall from grace and are replaced by modern monofilaments, there is no need for the most fastidious British angler to fit anything but tough Fuji and Hopkins & Holloway lined rings. Fuji CRHG are excellent. If you insist on rollers, pick Aftco or Mildrum.

Ring sizes are a debateable choice according to whether the rod will be used with multiplier reel, fixed spool or both. Provided they allow free passage of leader knots, multiplier rings have no advantage being huge. A 25–30 mm butt plus graduated intermediates suits the majority of surf rods, light and heavy. Much the same applies to traditional and uptide boat rods, but you need fewer rings to suit the blank.

Some anglers swear by small butt rings for fixed spool casting as well, the theory being that large coils of line flowing from the spool are quickly flattened and controlled. Others say that the ring should be at least 40 mm diameter to prevent excessive friction. Most of these theories are unproven; but many experienced anglers prefer to stick with a 50 mm butt ring simply because it reduces the odds of the leader knot tying itself around the ring frame.

Intermediates are again graded towards the tip to form an open cone or funnel. Most favoured types are Fuji BSHG and BNHG, big Seymos and Dynaflos. Specialist tournament casters sometimes use hardchromed wire rings of 75 mm or more diameter. They use wire because no other rings are made in such enormous sizes.

Ring spacing

No two blanks are exactly alike; even those wrapped on the same mandrel can be marginally different in power and action.

Each blank requires its own individual ring spacings for maximum performance. The scope of this book is not wide enough to go much beyond general recommendations, but I include most of the important ideas on how to tune up your rods for top quality results. Ring spacing is a personal matter anyway – provided you follow the basic rules.

Some blank manufacturers like Normark and North Western suggest numbers, sizes and spacings for their range of blanks and kits. The amateur builder making his first ever rod may well find them useful. If you buy a blank from a tackle dealer who knows his job, he should be able to advise you or even show you how to proceed. He may have a rod built on the same model blank as yours, in which case it is simply a question of transferring measurements across.

Bear in mind though that in both cases you will be copying someone else's ideas and calculations. They may be experts, but *you* are building *your* rod. You may feel that one more or less ring on the tip would improve performance; perhaps another kind of ring is more appropriate for your style of casting?

Suppose you prefer to go your own way. First, find the spine of your blank. Nearly all blanks have a hard and a soft side, the harder side corresponding with the initial layers of cloth rolled on to the blank mandrel. The result is that almost all blanks are biased to bend more easily in one plane. Spining a blank is the process of aligning rings with that plane. How you line up the rings makes a lot of difference to a rod's performance and may even affect its lifespan.

As you sight along a blank, you will probably detect a slight curve at the tip. Some anglers worry about it, but that offset actually signifies a well made product. Sudden bends are what you worry about – they indicate a serious fault in the blank.

Dead straight blanks may well be perfectly sound, but some cheap rods are doctored at the production stage to ensure the straightness that many anglers insist upon. The trick is to raise the resin content and cut back on glass or carbon fibres.

Cheap carbon blanks of high resin content can be pinpointed by their relative heaviness and sloppy feel. Compared with high class carbon blanks they feel dull and powerless instead of steely. So check your blanks carefully before purchase.

It is easy to see the spine bias of a single piece blank. Sectional blanks are usually cut and spigotted before arriving at the tackle shop, and here you must take care to realign the sections with each other. The spine bias itself is less important than on single piece rods, but it pays slowly to rotate the tip on the butt until the entire rod looks nice and straight. Mark the tip's position on the spigot as the basis for ring alignment.

Why do manufacturer's not mark the spine of the products? It would save so much time and heartache. Until they do, learn to check your own blanks. The tip's slight curve is usually towards the spine – that is, the inside of the curve is the spine or stiff side.

Straight blanks are tested this way. Rest the butt on the floor, hold the tip with one hand, then press down on the centre with your free hand. Rotate the blank steadily until you feel the stiff and soft planes under your hand. Mark the spine position for later reference.

Alternatively, stand the butt on the ground and lean the tip against a plain wall. The

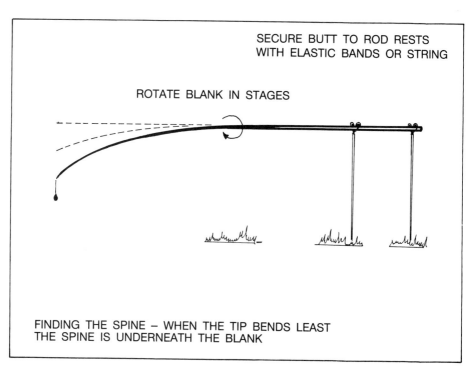

SECURE BUTT TO ROD RESTS
WITH ELASTIC BANDS OR STRING

ROTATE BLANK IN STAGES

FINDING THE SPINE – WHEN THE TIP BENDS LEAST
THE SPINE IS UNDERNEATH THE BLANK

Marking the spine.

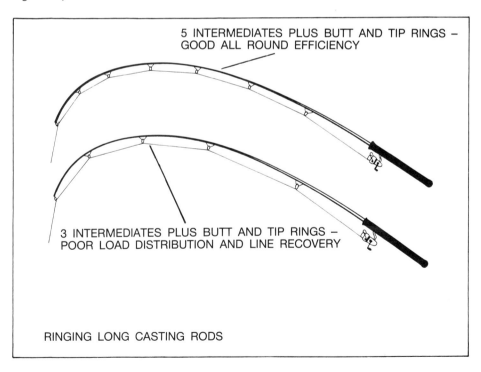

5 INTERMEDIATES PLUS BUTT AND TIP RINGS –
GOOD ALL ROUND EFFICIENCY

3 INTERMEDIATES PLUS BUTT AND TIP RINGS –
POOR LOAD DISTRIBUTION AND LINE RECOVERY

RINGING LONG CASTING RODS

blank will flip over and settle with its hard spine side facing the wall. If you are still in doubt, place two rod rests about 24 ins apart on the ground, secure the butt to the rests with elastic bands, and tie a short piece of line and lead weight to the extreme tip. Rotate the rod on the rests and note its plane of least bending. At that point the spine faces vertically downwards.

Spine alignment is not critical on light freshwater rods. You can whip rings to the hard or soft side, but not at right angles to them. That would ruin the rod action and tend also to loosen rings under the threads. It is customary to ring blanks on the outside of the spine curve (the soft side) so that the weight of rings offsets spine stiffness and results in a straight rod. Ringing on the soft side softens the action a little – perhaps not enough to influence performance – but does exaggerate the curve of the finished rod.

Blanks for long range casting in freshwater and salt should be ringed on the spine side. Fibres used in blank construction twist to follow the line of least resistance during the enormous strain of hard casting. Ringing on the soft side may result in fibres splitting. It is probably a minor risk; but why take chances?

Mark the spine plane, then tape the rings roughly into position according to maker's instructions or to your own theories. Tape the spigots as well. A few tight turns of masking tape protect them from the shock of test-casting. Now fit the reel and run line through the rings. Tie the end of the line to a convenient fence post and bend the rod into its fighting curve. Note the angle of line

A simple home-made whipping thread holder.

Marking position of ring centre.

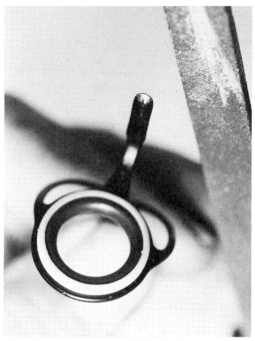

Ring feet must be filed smooth.

between the rings. Line should not touch the blank at any point, nor should it jump from ring to ring in oversize chords. Within reason, it should follow the blank's action curve.

It is unlikely you will hit the jackpot first time, or even second. Shift rings along the blank, add a few if necessary, or delete redundant ones. Experiment until you have the least number of rings that hold line in perfect harmony with the blank. In the case of blanks for multiplier reel work, rings are fitted on top and should be positioned so that no line touches the loaded rod. Multiplier boat blanks are kitted out the same way.

Tippy action rods need more rings where the blank bends most. Stiffer carp, pike and beach blanks use fewer, especially on the medium-fast taper models. Butt rings should be kept well away from the reel otherwise they choke line during the cast. As a rough guide, freshwater float butt rings must be at least 18 ins away from the reel; 24–26 ins suits leger rods for tench, barbel, pike and carp; add an extra few inches for long range casting rods. Beach butt rings must be at least 30 ins away from a multiplier and, within reason, as far as possible from a fixed spool. 36–40 ins is the absolute mininum for good casting.

Long range fixed spool rods throw the tackle a little farther if intermediate rings are reduced to a bare minimum. Friction is reduced enough to add a few extra yards to the cast. But at what cost to handling big fish? This season I persuaded some carp to assist in my experiments. Yes, too few rings do detract from the rod's fighting power. As ring numbers are decreased, so the line angle between rings increases under load to the point where they distribute the pressure unevenly on the blank and may inflict localised over-stress. Bad loading means poor performance – you can feel it with a good fish on. Line recovery becomes rough and the tackle threatens to lock at times.

Some compromise between casting and fishing is inevitable. Five intermediates plus butt and tip provide marginally better distances yet preserve even loading and good line control. The same formula ensures good dual purpose ringing for beach rods used with both fixed spool and multiplier reels. It does not matter if line touches lightly against the blank when the rod is loaded hard while fishing the multiplier.

Whipping

With the handle and reel fittings in place, ring types determined and spacing/spine calculations complete, we come to the easy job of whipping the blank. You will need whipping thread, Sellotape, a small file, a bottle of whipping sealer and a tube of hotmelt glue.

Gudebrod NCP is the world's favourite whipping thread. Unlike cheaper threads which produce a hairy, uneven whipping, Gudebrod is completely smooth; moreover it is colourfast and does not require sealing with colour preservative. Grade A is fine thread suited to coarse and fly rods; thicker grade D is best for sea tackle. Gudebrod is available in a wide range of colours and a variety of sizes. Most economical are 1200 yd and 575 yd spools – more than enough thread for a year's serious home building. Hold surplus in reserve for replacing broken rings. Gudebrod is a little more expensive than ordinary thread but

more than justifies the extra outlay.

Talbot thread is the only comparable British product. Usually supplied in smaller reels – from 50 yds upward – it is now available ready impregnated with colour sealer. In addition to standard colours, the Talbot range includes patterned threads that give whippings a two-tone effect. Not every tackle dealer stocks Talbot but North Western Blanks distribute the range. So, if you can't find a local supply, contact them direct.

Ring whipping is easy enough, yet the job can be awkward without a convenient rest to hold the rod steady. I used to muddle through by resting the blank across the arms of a chair but now use a pair of simple wooden frames padded with chunks of foam which protect the blank surface. Keen do-it-yourself men rig up wooden devices incorporating a steel pin or nail that holds the thread spool. Failing that, drop the bobbin into a mug to stop it rolling across the floor; better still, wind thread on to a multiplier reel. Clutch tension is adjusted until thread pulls off at exactly the right tension to produce a perfect whipping.

Ring feet should be prepared before whipping takes place, otherwise the thread forms an unsightly step as it climbs from blank to ring. If the ends of the feet are blunt – and they will be on cheap rings – file them down to a smooth taper. Avoid making them so pointed that the ring foot might dig into the blank when the rod is under pressure. Even top quality rings need a little preparation in this department.

It matters not whether you whip a rod from tip to butt or the other way around. Some prefer to glue on the tip first and use it as a guide for aligning the rest of the rings. Others like myself start with the butt ring and use that as the reference point for the others. Peer through it as if it were a

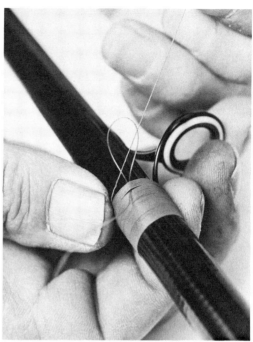

Sellotape rings into position.

Complete the whipping and tuck the end of the thread into the nylon loop.

unsight, and if necessary tweak the rest into line.

First step is to cut a small section of Sellotape and tape down one foot of the butt ring. Make sure the ring sits squarely on the blank and directly over the mark determined in ring spacing tests. Don't forget to align the ring with the blank's spine.

With the butt ring in place, decide how wide you want each whipping to be. Foot width plus about $\frac{3}{16}$ in each side is about right - and you can mark those points with a ruler and pencil. Some experienced builders can judge whippings by eye, but to start with it pays to measure each one. An alternative method is to count the number of turns of thread lying beyond the ring foot, then duplicate them on the other side whipping. Both sides of each individual ring should be

whipped the same way. Decrease the overhang in step with falling ring sizes as you work your way up the blank.

Whip up the foot rather than down to the blank. This technique helps avoid any gap in the whippings as the thread climbs the foot. Whipping down is apt to cause thread slip on the larger rings particularly. Begin whipping by taking a couple of turns of thread around the blank, trapping the first of them with the third turn, then laying subsequent turns neatly side by side. Moistening the end of the thread provides enough anchorage for an easy start to the coils.

Lay on about a dozen coils, then trim back the under-tucked loose end. Continue to whip by holding the thread steady between finger and thumb while you rotate the blank. Apply moderate tension to keep the ring

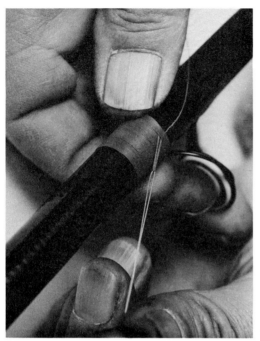

Pull the end of the thread under the main coils of whipping.

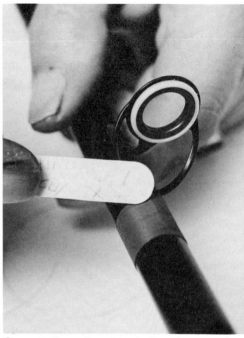

Smooth the coils with a knife edge or strip of hard plastic.

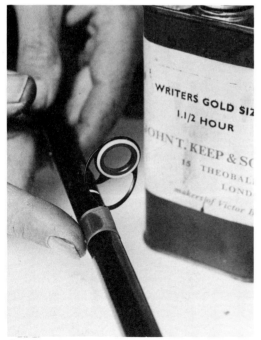

Sealing and gluing threads with writer's gold size.

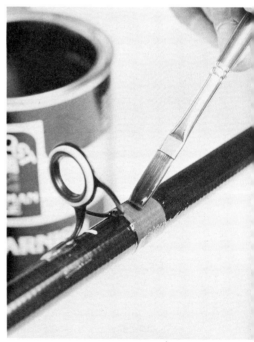

Varnish is both an adhesive and a decorative seal.

anchored in position. However, do avoid excessive thread pressure: thin-walled glass and carbon blanks could be cracked by too much thread tension.

Keep tension moderate and even, and lay each turn snugly against its neighbour. The idea is to produce a neat coil of thread, not to seal the ring in place. Adhesives applied later do that. Continue to whip up the ring foot, putting the thread snugly as you go. Good quality thread lays itself into place almost automatically as you spin the blank. Tiny gaps are corrected later on, but big ones must be unwound and rewhipped now.

Stop whipping when the threads lie within six turns or so of the end. Insert a loop of line as shown in the pictures (monofilament is best) and after laying in the final turns of whipping, snip the thread, feed the end through the loop, and pull the loop back under the whipping coils. This simple trick tucks the end of the whipping neatly under itself for security. Carefully trim the loose end with a sharp razor blade. With luck the whipping will look perfect.

Even new razor blades can leave a tiny lump where the thread is trimmed. Credit goes to that excellent rod builder Terry Eustace for an improved and only slightly more difficult whip finish that solves the problem entirely. With this method you insert the nylon loop earlier than normal – say before the final fifteen turns drop into position. Finish laying on the thread as previously described, cut the thread and push it into the loop, then pull the loop a little way under the fifteen coils. Now trim back the loose end of thread, so that when you pull

All joints must be whipped before you use the rod.

Label your rod with white paint or dry transfer lettering.

71

again on the loop the cut end stays inside the whipping.

With the first foot whipped, remove Sellotape from the other side of the ring, sight along the blank to make sure the ring is correctly aligned, then add the second whipping. Continue to work along the blank, whipping and adjusting each intermediate in turn. Remember that the rings must be aligned with themselves *and also with the blank's spine*.

Single-leg rings are whipped the same way. Use a sliver of Sellotape to hold the foot down while you get the thread started, then take it off and whip your way over the foot.

When whipping large rings on sea rods there is no objection to leaving a piece of Sellotape on each foot and covering it with thread. As a matter of fact this helps prevent a step forming when the thread climbs off the blank and up the ring.

Underwrapping is another way to increase ring security on heavy saltwater blanks. Whip a band of thread across the blank section where the ring sits, tape on the ring, then apply the foot wraps as normal.

Assuming you started ringing at the butt, it is now time to glue on the tip ring with a dab of hotmelt glue. As its name implies, this adhesive is melted on to the blank and the tip is pressed on and held still until the glue cools and sets hard. The great advantage is that broken rings can be removed in an instant by heating the metal support tube with a match. You can change rings at the waterside if necessary. Araldite or any other epoxy adhesive does an equally good bonding job but may be impossible to soften without harming the blank. Many blanks are themselves held together by an epoxy matrix. Make sure the tip ring aligns with the intermediates and the blank's spine. A small whipping applied at the ring

tube base completes a professional job.

All rings are in place, so now it is time to reinforce the spigot with a broad, tight whipping on each side of the joint, or in the case of an overfit joint, to cover the female end with thread. Spigots are subject to considerable stress and whipping strengthens the danger area. Whip at least 1½ ins either side of the joint on freshwater rods, 2 ins for long range models, and at least 3 ins on beachcasters.

Short trims of contrasting colour applied either end of ring and spigot whippings add that final touch to a good rod. Since only four or five turns of thread are used for the trim it is easier to lay the loop on to the blank then whip all the turns over it before cutting and pulling under as you did on the main whipping. Tidy the trim and push it neatly against the main whipping.

No matter how carefully you apply whippings, slight gaps exist where threads did not fall into exactly the right spot. They are soon closed and smoothed by rubbing lightly with the reverse side of a knife blade or even with a fingernail. Do this to all the whips before applying sealer.

Sealing the whippings

Whipping dope is usually used to seal threads and preserve colour. It is not necessary on Gudebrod thread or on the new Talbot nylon material so far as colour preservation is concerned, but it does fill the threads and make them neater. Dope has the unfortunate habit of sometimes turning the threads into a whitish mess. This happens only now and again, but once is too much when you have spent hours assembling a fine rod.

Plain varnish alone can be used to stick down light freshwater rings and sea whippings to a smooth finish. Gold size is even better. This varnish-like liquid is adhesive and has slightly more body than varnish. Size is used by signwriters to glue down gold leaf, and is available in various drying times from 1½–24 hrs. Good paint stockists and art shops should have it. The longer the drying time, the more durable results will be. 12 hr size is recommended for rod building.

Several coats are needed; care and patience at this stage will ensure a good finish later. Wipe varnish or size on to the whippings with a fingertip, and do not be afraid to saturate the threads; be sure to rub plenty into those that lie over the step between blank and ring foot. Leave varnish or size to dry for at least 24 hrs; it must be completely hard before you proceed, otherwise the rod's appearance will be ruined.

The next step is to smooth whippings with gentle strokes of extra fine sandpaper. Whisk away furry patches and whiskers of thread. Top quality whipping threads demand very little smoothing, but some of the cheap brands look like a hairy doormat. Brush away dust and apply a second coat of varnish, again with your fingertip. Leave it to dry for the recommended time. Repeat rhe exercise.

Epoxy resin rod coating products are excellent provided you keep the blank rotating while the material cures.

Three coats of varnish stick the rings into position but may not be sufficient to fill threads. Continue with another two, three, or even four coats until the whippings are sealed under a gloss finish. Do not rush the job – success depends on leaving undercoats to dry thoroughly.

Yes, rod finishing is tedious. You could stop at just one coat of varnish or size, but the rod will never look good and the rings would loosen within a few weeks. Quality is the target, and that takes time to achieve. Never apply quick drying cellulose-based sealers on top of ordinary size or varnish. Varnish may be applied on top of cellulose, but never the other way around because cellulose solvents eat away varnish, resulting in a sticky, bubbly mess which cannot be rectified without stripping the blank back to bare glass or carbon.

The multi-coat varnish/size method ensures a good finish and has been found perfectly adequate for fixing rings to light freshwater rods. But there are quicker ways to complete your rod by using special adhesives. These are essential for cementing rings on to heavier freshwater and sea tackle.

Transparent adhesives like Bostik or Uhu can be employed to stick down the threads. Wipe a smear on to the whippings with your finger, but do work quickly or the glue will gel before it sinks into the nylon strands. Araldite epoxy glue can be used the same way, and it provides a strong key for big rings on saltwater blanks. Mix together a drop of adhesive and hardener in a tin lid, and heat the glue over boiling water until it thins down and becomes runny enough to be painted or rubbed into the threads. One coat should be enough to stick down rings, fill threads and build a smooth, glossy shell over the whipping. Alternatively, apply one coat of Araldite then switch to the standard varnish/size routine.

Special two part epoxy resins are much favoured by professional rod builders. Epoxy offers excellent adhesion, sealing and filling properties and can be applied rapidly. Sometimes a single coat completes the sealing process. Such products are not readily available and they are expensive.

These epoxy rod finishes demand more careful application than varnish and size. The liquid is applied liberally, and the blank must be rotated slowly until the material gels. This can be done by hand but is far more convenient on motorised frames. Gudebrod Hard-N-Fast marketed by Masterline stockists is excellent. (If difficulties arise contact them at Cotswold Road Tewkesbury, Gloucestershire.)

Varnishing the rod

Many blanks are sold with a durable finish already applied, so further coats are not strictly necessary. Most home builders prefer to add a coat or two which builds up an even better gloss finish. The work is easy, and good results are guaranteed if you remember to check the rod beforehand.

The rod will almost certainly be covered with smears and fingermarks, so the first step is to rub down the blank and fittings with methylated spirits which cleans components, shifts grease and also keys the surface for varnish.

Work in a dust-free room if you can. The bathroom is best, but failing that the kitchen will do. Whatever happens, you must not allow specks of dust to fall on the newly coated rod – so declare your work place a people-free zone for the interim.

Most clear varnishes look nice when fresh, but few last long. Polyurethane particularly soon deteriorates because its hard shell flakes under the constant flexing of the blank. Longer lasting finishes are obtained with oil based varnishes that dry to form a more rubbery skin which moves with the rod.

I have experimented with mixtures of linseed oil and varnish. The result is a much tougher finish, but takes ages to dry. The mixture is recommended if you have plenty of time to build a rod. Add one part of boiled linseed oil to three parts varnish. Drying speeds up on the addition of a little paint driers. Careful though . . . too much driers makes varnish brittle.

Ordinary clear oil copal gloss varnish is probably the best, with or without linseed oil added. Some people use yacht varnish with good results. And if you must use polyurethane, choose Ronseal which is more flexible than most brands.

The specialist two part epoxies also produce superb high gloss, durable finishes. However, they are quick to go wrong unless you have the experience and equipment to apply them correctly. Unsightly blobs and drips that ruin whippings can just as easily mar the blank itself. Mix the two chemicals exactly as recommended and keep the rod moving until the epoxy gels firmly enough not to run.

Quite the best idea I have heard on rod finishing comes from John Holden who recommends a few coats of Turtle Wax Formula 3 polymer car wax applied to blank, rings and to epoxy-sealed whippings. No need to wait for varnish to dry, or to worry about dust and drips. The wax produces a high gloss, tough shine and needs only

Polymer car wax rubbed on to blank and whippings produces a tough, shiny finish with no need for varnish or epoxy.

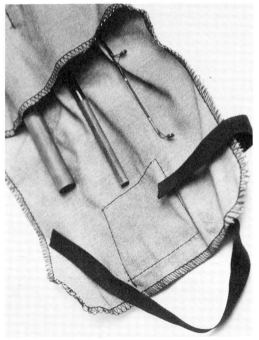

A rod bag adds that final touch of quality and protects slim blank sections.

occasional repolishing to retain its quality.

Now and again, somebody comes up with advice about varnishing a rod by fingertip. In my opinion you should not do it. The method may have originated from the days of built cane where, because of the hexagonal section, fingertips do produce the best results. Modern round blanks give nowhere near such a smooth and even finish unless you do use a brush.

A *good* brush is essential. Don't even bother to try a cheap one; it will not spread the varnish evenly and is sure to leave hairs all over the rod. Ask your local art shop for a chisel edge ¼in Dalon brush. It has synthetic bristles, gives fine results and is relatively cheap. Or buy an ox hair brush – it is at least as good and costs only a little more.

The first coat of varnish should be thin and smooth. Work with even brush strokes down the blank, and be sure you miss nothing. Tease varnish into awkward spots below rings. I usually begin at the tip and work back to the handle, one section at a time. It helps to stick a pen into the female spigot joints so that you can hold the blank when no dry areas of glass or carbon remain. It also supports the section while the varnish dries.

Do not be tempted to apply the second coat for at least 24 hrs after which the rod should be lightly rubbed down if necessary. Use the finest grade of sandpaper – and make sure to wipe off the resulting dust.

Apply the second coat as before, but work more freely with a well loaded brush. High quality brushes ensure easy application and fine results. Leave that to dry, then go for a third coat. Four coats are even better and

five coats are the hallmark of the best professional builders.

If you prefer a matt finish, apply matt varnish on top of two or three gloss coats. Sand the penultimate coat to key the surface otherwise the matt will not take so well. Matt varnish has a short life anyway. You can delay the discolouration and flaking by brushing on a half-and-half mixture of matt and gloss varnishes instead.

Why not personalise your new rod with your name? Dream up a suitable name for the rod itself – '12 ft Mk.1 Carpseeker' perhaps. Lettering adds that final touch and makes the rod much easier to identify in the case of light fingers.

Personalising is better done before final varnishing. White lettering looks best on black and dark hued blanks; try black letters on yellow and light toned rods. If you are artistic, write directly on the blank with white paint and a fine brush, or Tippex and a mapping pen. Black ink is fine for light blanks, but unfortunately white drawing ink is far too pale for rod labelling.

Letraset dry transfer lettering is superb. Letters are available in a vast range of colours, sizes and styles. Buy a sheet from art shops or office suppliers. It is expensive but worthwhile on top quality fishing rods.

All that remains is to let the rod stand for a couple of days to harden. Buy a good rod bag to protect it . . . and go fishing. Remember to look after your varnishing brushes though. Wash the bristles and handle in turpentine substitute to swill away all traces of varnish. Cellulose based dopes must be cleaned of the brush with cellulose thinners; turps is no good.

MAINTENANCE, REPAIRS AND SPLICING

MAINTENANCE AND REPAIRS

A sensible maintenance programme keeps your new rod in perfect condition. Wipe it down after each session to remove bits of groundbait and grime. Pay special attention to rings on the tip section which pick up floating scum and debris as a result of continually being dunked in order to sink line after casting. Neglected tips attract a hard coat of grime around the ring frames that is difficult to remove. An old toothbrush is useful for cleaning otherwise inaccessible spots.

Dirty, groundbait clogged hands transfer their muck to handle corks. These are easily cleaned by lightly scrubbing with household detergent. After a couple of seasons you can completely restore the original cork sheen by light sanding with fine paper. Do not overdo it though — there is no sense in ending up with loose reel fittings.

If, like me, you develop the habit of sticking hooks into the top of the cork handle while you move swims, you will not complain when those insignificant prick marks grow into deep, ugly scars. These are cured by a layer of plastic wood or a dose of the cork dust/glue filler previously described. Better still, whip a keeper ring to the rod butt and use that to park your hook.

Beach and boat rods need rather more care due to the inroad of corrosive saltwater.

Salt eats metal; sea rods tend to receive more knocks and abuse because of the rigours of the sport itself. A regular wash down together with a spray of WD40 on rings and fittings keep your rod in perfect condition.

With the best care in the world, a hard used rod will look a shade dog eared after one season's fishing. An annual wipe down with fine sandpaper followed by a top-up coat of varnish bring it up like new. Alternatively, use regular applications of tough car polish such as Turtle Wax Formula 3.

It is a wise precaution to check both sides of a spigot joint for dirt, sand and grit before assembling the rod. Gone unnoticed, even one grain of sand scratches both mating surfaces. A few scratches are not serious, but repeated neglect causes damage that cannot be repaired. Dirty male spigots are obvious and are easily cleaned with a cloth, but grit can remain hidden inside a female joint. Develop the habit of blowing into the spigot before setting up the rod. Some anglers even carry a small brush to swish out loose muck.

The safest course is to stop dirt creeping inside in the first place. Buy or make plugs that fit into the female section when the rod is not in use. Once all high quality rods were sold with ferrule plugs to safeguard the joints – an idea well worth reviving by the tackle trade.

Badly scored male spigots are partially restored by rubbing on and polishing in several coats of hard beeswax. Regular waxing does no harm anyway, and manufacturers of some top-brand carbonfibre rods insist that the angler maintains a slick of wax on spigots to ensure long life. Ordinary candle wax is adequate for routine protection but lacks the body to fill scratches. A coat of graphite (pencil lead will do) on the male also ensures a non-stick joint and prevents excessive wear.

Graphited or waxed spigots last for years, but eventually the small gap deliberately left between sections by the manufacturer closes up. Spigots loosen and rattle, and in

this condition are much more likely to sna under sudden pressure. Cure the fault b trimming back the female side to restore th $\frac{1}{4}$ in gap necessary for perfect spigot fi Remember to replace the protective ove whip.

Replacement of broken tip rings is a fiv minute job if you originally used Gudebrod o Fuji hot-melt adhesive. Insulate the ro below the tip ring with plenty of tape, hol the ring near a low gas flame until it pulls of the end of the blank. Apply more hot-melt t the blank, and press a new ring into position

The neatest way to replace intermediat rings is carefully to cut off the whipping remove the ring and then whip a new on into exactly the same position, making sur the new threads settle over the original are When coating the whipping, feather a fev

Regular spraying with Teflon or WD40 maintains saltwater tackle in top condition for at least 18 months.

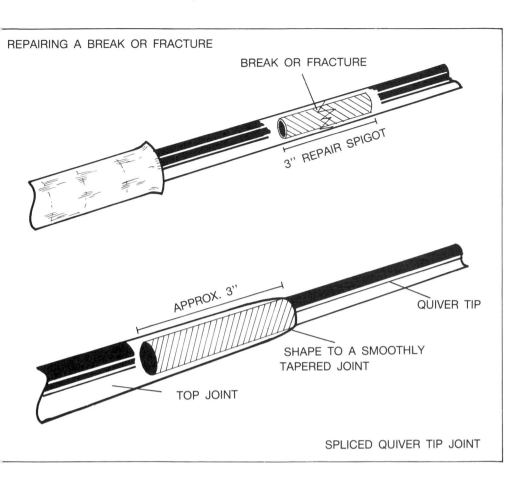

REPAIRING A BREAK OR FRACTURE

BREAK OR FRACTURE

3" REPAIR SPIGOT

APPROX. 3"

QUIVER TIP

SHAPE TO A SMOOTHLY
TAPERED JOINT

TOP JOINT

SPLICED QUIVER TIP JOINT

ches of fresh varnish along the blank to
end with the old.

The foregoing are simple jobs requiring
tle time and effort. However, accidents do
appen. Rods are trodden on or shut in car
oors. Tips break or crack by inadvertently
abbing into the ground. Sometimes a
eavy fish suddenly dives into the bank and
verloads the blank.

Repairing major damage like this depends
here the fault lies and how seriously it has
tten into the blank's fabric. Damage in the
p third of a rod calls for replacement of the
hole section. Most rod factories will
upply a matched section provided you
ther identify the blank specification
umber or send the lower sections to them
r hand-fitting a replacement part. Any
tempt to repair a tip inevitably fails.

Butts and middle sections are certainly
worth repairing. The resulting flat spot in
action is less severe than if it were at the tip.
The nearer the butt, the more viable the
repair becomes; and on some of the more
powerful surfcasting rods, a repaired handle
section may not affect action in the least.

Clean breaks are easier to repair than
cracks. Most extensive cracks that open up
several inches of the blank fibres are not
worth attempting to repair but a single
hairline crack can be cured by no more than a
substantial length of whipping cemented
with plenty of epoxy and varnish.

Clean snaps and short, ragged fractures
are remedied by underpinning them with an
internal spigot section tapered to match the
inner blank walls. Overlap the damaged
section by $\frac{3}{4}$ in at both ends; that is, a 3 in

crack needs a $4\frac{1}{2}$ in insert.

Your tackle dealer may happen to have a suitable piece of glassfibre or carbon. Ideally, choose a piece long enough to insert beyond the damage and stil protrude far enough for easy withdrawal. Use a shorter piece if you must . . . and if it disappears up the broken joint, just turn the blank over and tap the walls until the offender pops out. This is one good reason not to glue on butt caps in the first place.

Match the insert against the damaged section, mark off the appropriate length, add an extra 2 ins at the thick end of the taper and cut through with hacksaw or file. Insert the spigot again and wiggle it around to determine how closely it matches the inner blank taper. Sand or carefully file the insert to fit snugly, then make. a final length adjustment to produce the necessary $\frac{3}{4}$ in overlap.

Glue the insert with Araldite or similar adhesive. Use warmed adhesive which flows smoothly and easily. Coat the spigot and drop it into the blank. With the help of a suitable ramrod, push the insert into place, then slide on the broken upper section of blank. *Do not use excessive pressure or too much adhesive*, both of which may damage the blank still more. Clean off drips of Araldite, ensure that cracks themselves are filled with glue, then leave the repair to harden. Afterwards, clean off with fine sandpaper, whip the fractured section, seal and varnish.

SPLICING A TIP JOINT

Most blanks with spliced in tips are supplied complete and ready to build, but it helps t know how to carry out the work for yourse Then you can buy ordinary freshwate blanks and modify them for speci purposes.

If your rod is carbon, insist on a carbo spliced section to match. Normark supp the best solid carbon tips in lengths fro 320 mm to 885 mm, the longer ones fo match rods and the short pieces for quive leger rods. Glass tops and 'donkey tops' a available for ordinary glassfibre rods.

First cut a section from the tip joint. Tri back cautiously because you cannot replac material afterwards. Use a sharp hacksa for cutting glassfibre and a fine-toothed fi for carbonfibre. Now drop the splice into th bottom of the tip joint so that it pops out o the cut end. If it does not protrude fa enough, take it out and cut back the ro blank a litle farther. Repeat the exercise un the splice extends the correct distanc Mark the splice at the base of its protrusio take it out of the rod tip, measure dow another three inches from the mark, and cu off the excess.

The top joint itself must be ground to taper for at least 3 ins to ensure a smoot through action at the joint. Do that ve carefully with a sharp file and a sandin block. Then work some warm Araldite int the tapered section of top joint, and drop th spliced section into place through the blar bottom. Be very careful how you feed th splice into position. The tapered end of th main blank will split if you pull too har Guide it gently through the hole until th previously made mark appears. Clean o surplus glue, leave to dry, then whip over th spliced section for added security.